Brad Stanley believes the city is holy Promised Land. I agree. When we p... ... ., we should not be surprised the nations come to us. If we can't or won't go to them, God brings them to our doorstep so the great commission can be fulfilled and the heart of God made known to a paralyzed church and a lost people.

Migrations to cities are taking place, not just to cities in their own lands, but a vast, eclectic disapora of cultures and ethnicities are piling into cities from one continent to another. This is good. It is God's doing. In Brad's words, it is a modern day miracle. People from hundreds of unreached people groups are moving to cities where the gospel is readily available and the church is reaching out.

Just as there were divinely appointed "cities of refuge" in the Old Testament, so God has appointed cities to have certain roles, or "anointings" if you will, today. He gives individuals, nations and cities callings to fulfill His plan of redemption and transformation.

When that calling goes unfulfilled it creates a spiritual vacuum, and the city declines. Without obedience, a city and nation makes room for the enemy to hold sway. To look at the fallen city without seeing it through God's eyes, is to miss the purposes of God. Far too many people see the sin but not the unfulfilled covenant and broken promises of God over a city.

Finding God in the City is a moving, faith building, eye opening call to see how God sees. When Jesus saw Jerusalem and wept over the city, He mourned what could and should have been. What He saw affected what he felt. This book will enable you to do the same, to see and feel and think as Jesus does.

I highly commend it. It is a prophetic voice, calling us with tears and wisdom back to the heart of God.

—Floyd McClung
All Nations
Cape Town, South Africa

If we are going to see the world come to Christ then we need to see thousands of young people take up the challenges of living, ministering and transforming neighborhoods and cities. More than 50 percent of the world lives in small, medium and mega cities around the world and the trend of the world moving to urban areas continues. Brad has the experience and track record to help show us how to do that. His passion for the unreached and his heart to know God in the midst of the urban jungle will inspire you to see the city as God sees it. If you are called to work in a city amongst the poor, the unreached, the upper class, the street kids, drug addicts or business people Brad's book *Finding God in the City* is for you. Brad Stanley has inspired me to dig my feet deeper into the challenges that living in a city presents. If you want a challenge that is bigger than you then read Brad's book and let God speak to you about how he can use you in the city.

—Tim Svoboda
YWAM San Francisco
and Bay Area Coordinator
YWAM International Cities Director

Fresh thoughts! Timely and very motivating! A must read for urban practitioners! Strong blend of stats, calling, Scripture and reaching the nations in our cities. Brad has earned the scars to write this book. He exhorts us to truly be a generation of urban

Christians and reminds us that our Lord is at work in the city! God help us to heed your admonition and example of over two decades of selfless service. We hear you, and your YWAM comrades Brother! Keep on!

—Dr. John Fuder
Director, Justice and Compassion Ministries
Author, *A Heart for the City*

Brad and I have known each other for the last ten years and share a common call to reach the ethnic peoples of the world. He has led me by the hand into the rich, diverse neighborhoods of Chicago that he has written about. Together we are planting a multi-ethnic church in the epicenter of these 150 nations. He is still leading me by the heart to see an urban mission revival among these miracle near nations. This prophetic book is a must read for every believer and will be a new standard textbook for modern mission!

—Dick Bashta
Pastor, Living Stones ChicaGO
Director, GlobalROAR

FINDING GOD IN THE CITY

BRAD STANLEY

CREATION
HOUSE

Finding God in the City:
Making Sense of an Urban World by Brad Stanley
Published by Creation House
A Charisma Media Company
600 Rinehart Road
Lake Mary, Florida 32746
www.charismamedia.com

Unless otherwise noted, all Scripture quotations are from the Holy Bible, New International Version of the Bible. Copyright © 1973, 1978, 1984, International Bible Society. Used by permission.

Scripture quotations marked esv are from the Holy Bible, English Standard Version, Copyright © 2001 by Crossway Bibles, a division of Good News Publishers. Used by permission.

Scripture quotations marked kjv are from the King James Version of the Bible.

Scripture quotations marked nkjv are from the New King James Version of the Bible. Copyright © 1979, 1980, 1982 by Thomas Nelson, Inc., publishers. Used by permission.

Some names have been changed in order to preserve and protect the anonymity of the individuals involved.

Design Director: Bill Johnson
Cover design by Nathan Morgan

Visit the author's website: www.findinggodinthecity.com

Library of Congress Cataloging-in-Publication Data: 2011936195
International Standard Book Number: 978-1-61638-690-0
E-book International Standard Book Number:
978-1-61638-691-7

First edition

11 12 13 14 15 — 987654321
Printed in Canada

Dedication

To the first Urban Generation and those who long to carry that distinction with vision and purpose.

ACKNOWLEDGEMENTS

URING EVERY CULTURAL shift, as well as in modern mission movements, there have been prophetic and pioneering voices. The same has been true in the last fifty years as the world experienced the phenomenon of global urbanization. It has been my hope to both honor some of those voices as well as introduce them to a new generation, having adopted the very thing they prophetically spoke about. These pioneers of urban vision have included men like Roger Greenway, Harvie Conn, and Ray Bakke, who were willing to dream for the city when much of church culture sought a way to get out. It included men like Floyd McClung, John Dawson, and Jack Dennison who called us to believe in what God could do in the city. Men like John Perkins and Wayne Gordon showed us that even the most troubled neighborhoods could be transformed by the presence of God's people.

All of these men have inspired me by their vision and practical faith as they spoke about a world becoming urban and what we could do as God's people in that environment. I have quoted many of them throughout the book and have included many of their books in the bibliography. Their books sit on my shelves along with many others that I have not mentioned. My gratitude is immense for those men and women who marked out a trail of vision toward the city that this millennial generation is now able to run on.

I am grateful for the staff that has co-labored with me

in Youth With A Mission Chicago for the last twenty years. We have dreamt together, wept together, and enjoyed an amazing adventure with Jesus together. Thank you for inspiring me to continue in the call of God on my family and helping to provide the grace that we needed along the way. I am grateful for Ron and Evelyn Moyer, who, as my closest friends, always seem to give me the faith to do more than what I think is possible. A special thanks goes to Ruth Troyer for her help in the early editing process. I am thankful for my wife, Sherry, who, though she is with Jesus now, was able to instill in me more vision for the city and its people in the short time I had with her than anyone I know. If she were still here, it most assuredly would be her writing this book more than me. And most importantly, I am thankful for the two amazing kids the Lord has given me. Jordan and Joseph not only inspire me with the way they have made the city their home, but in whose generation I see all that is needed to unlock the gift of the city in ways no other generation has been able to do.

TABLE OF CONTENTS

INTRODUCTION

R IGHT NOW, AS you read this, the world is experiencing the greatest migration in human history. Global urbanization is happening at more than twice that of annual population growth,[1] and cities are growing at a rate of 1.6 million a week.[2] In 2008 the first urban generation came into existence with more than 50 percent of the world's population now living in cities. On a BBC urbanization website, you can watch a ticker calculating the growth of cities globally, with approximately three people per second moving into a city.[3] According to the United Nations 2009 report on world urbanization prospects, all projections for rural populations globally will see negative growth annually for the next four decades.[4] If the current trend continues, 60 percent of the world will live in cities in twenty years, nearly 70 percent in forty years,[5] and an estimated 90 percent of the world by the end of the century.[6] The twenty-first century will go down in history as the century of global urbanization. Yet according to *National Geographic*, the rate at which cities are growing is one of the four major challenges of our time, along with mutating diseases, global famine pandemics, and loss of fresh water supply.[7]

Nearly all of the world's governments and humanitarian organizations have concluded that global urbanization is a phenomenon that no one is prepared for. The growth of megacities around the globe has seemed to expose and exploit every problem known to man. As these cities grow bigger, so do the violence, poverty, and social injustice. Most countries of the world are adopting population control techniques and urbanization reversal strategies to slow down this phenomenon. Yet it doesn't seem to work; rather the rate of migration continues to escalate. The global urban population is expected to double in thirty-nine years, making the number of people living in cities by 2040 equal to the entire population of the globe in 2004.[8]

Though cities have been a part of man's history for thousands of years, the current phenomenon is marked by the explosive growth of cities worldwide and the rate at which every nation is urbanizing. An explosion of urbanization marked the twentieth century in Western cultures. Yet what it took the West to do in 150 years, the developing world of Asia and Africa are doing in half the time. In 1950 there were only three cities in the developing world with little over five million people in them: Tokyo, Shanghai, and Buenos Aires. Today there are nearly fifty, with half of them near or more than ten million in size.[9]

In the last thirty years, sociologists have had to develop new terminology for the size of modern cities. In 1900 there were only twelve cities in the world with around one million people in them. As the number of cities grew, so did their size. By 1980 there were 216 "supercities" of one to ten million, and a new term, "megacity" was developed, with four cities having more than ten million inhabitants. By 2010 the world saw 440 supercities and 20 megacities. However the megacities had become so large that a new phenomenon had developed called the "agglomeration." Some cities had grown to the point that they were now engulfing all their surrounding cities, producing one massive urban sprawl. An example would be the agglomeration of Tokyo, Japan, which has reached over thirty-six million, engulfing eighty-seven surrounding cities and towns.[10] According to the United Nations, if it were a country, it would rank thirty-fifth in population surpassing the populations of Algeria, Canada, and Uganda. In the next six years, China will finish a massive infrastructure development that will connect nine neighboring cities into the largest megacity agglomeration in the world, with forty-two million people.[11]

It's hard to imagine a city with tens of millions of people living in it unless you are from that environment. Today there are dozens of cities in the developing world growing by 200,000 to 400,000 annually.[12] That's a group the size of Minneapolis moving into a city every year. I remember visiting one such city, Mumbai, India, several years ago for the first time. Already at 20 million, it is expected to grow by 400,000 a year for the next fifteen years. The magnitude of this growth sunk in one day when our small team went to the nearby public train station needing to get to the other side of the city. I entered what looked like several football stadiums. In it were dozens of different train platforms. We found our number, stood on the appropriate platform, and waited alongside about a hundred other passengers for the train. What followed was the most amazing sight I had ever seen.

As the train began to come into our platform I noticed two things. First, there were people hanging all over the train, outside windows, open doors, and even on top of the train. Second, I noticed people jumping off of the train before it even came to a stop. This seemed to be necessitated by the fact that the hundred or so standing on the platform were running and trying to jump on the train at the same time. Our small team stood there in amazement. By the time the train stopped in front of us there was no possible way to get on. The platform was already filling up with another one hundred or so people waiting to get on the next train that arrived.

How do you manage a city like this? How do you provide housing, food, and sanitary conditions for so many people moving into your city every day? In *Urban Ministry*, Conn and Ortiz point out, "It's estimated that half the urban populations of Africa, Asia, and Latin America live in slums. Africa's cities have become what one author has called 'centers of despair.'"[13] Added to this is the fact that those moving to the city daily are from sometimes hundreds of different linguistic and ethnic groups, rural farming cultures, and impoverished countrysides. According to the United Nations, the leading factors for indigenous peoples increasingly moving to urban areas are things like forcible removal and displacement, wars, poverty, natural disasters, and the hope of employment opportunities. These are all high-need situations. What are increasingly pouring into cities around the world are people desperate for survival, safety, and a possible future better than what they had left behind. However, what they find is sometimes the very opposite.

Where is God in all of this? How does He feel about this migration? How does He feel about the city? As followers of Jesus, we believe that God is involved in our world. He is weaving a plan throughout history that involves reclaiming His original design and intent for all that He has created. What does global urbanization do to that plan? Is it at odds with what God is doing, or in cooperation? The answers to these questions have implications for the church. Not only do they dictate our attitude and approach toward the city but also the strategies we implement in response to urbanization worldwide. What changes do we have to make, if any, in response to a world where most people are increasingly living in cities?

Twenty-five years ago I sat in the window of a multiunit apartment building looking down on a busy city street in Chicago. There were a few odd things about this moment. It was 2:00 a.m. but the street was lit up and as busy as it would be in the afternoon, and I was a nineteen-year-old small-town kid from rural Texas. What I saw was as foreign to me as traveling to another country. I had joined Youth With A Mission almost a year earlier and was on a two-month outreach to Chicago. It was my shift to pray in our team's nighttime prayer vigil for the outreach. I enjoyed these meetings with God in the middle of the night. Though the city never seemed to sleep, it was at least a little quieter than normal. I prayed that God would give me His heart for the city. I tried to relate to the people I had seen throughout the day. But for the most part I felt out of place in the big city and intimidated by the overcrowded busyness of it all. I wasn't sure why anyone would want to live there.

And then the unthinkable happened. I heard God say to my heart that He lived there. Of course I knew that God loved the people in the city. I knew that He had compassion on them and wanted them to live in relationship with Himself. But for the most part I had seen the city as a hindrance to that goal. There was so much sin, rebellion, and violence in the city. It seemed to be the place people went in order to run from God, or at least live independently of Him. It was a rat race of humanity, exalting itself and often exploiting or abusing each other in endless pursuit of self-gratification. However, I didn't hear God say that He wanted to save as many out of the city as He could. That night, I sensed God saying that He actually lived in the city, that He felt at home in that environment, and wanted people to experience His presence there in a relational way.

Following this remarkable idea of God actually enjoying the city, something happened that has only happened a few times in my life. I heard God ask me a question. I had begun to recognize more and more what God's voice sounded like to my heart over the previous few years. Furthermore, I knew the question had to be from Him because the thought would have never entered my mind. I heard Him ask me if I would be willing to come and live in the city with Him. I was frightened by the question! First of all, living in a big North American city was not what I had signed up for. I wanted to be a missionary. I felt God's call on my life to take the gospel to the ends of the earth. I joined a movement of young people passionately wanting to finish the Great Commission and reach those who had never heard of Jesus. How did living in the third-largest city of the U.S. fit that goal? Secondly, I was frightened by the thought of why God would ask me a question unless He might want me to do the very thing He was asking. I felt trapped. If I said no, then it would mean I was not willing to follow Him any-where. However, if I said yes, then it might mean He was indeed going to ask me to spend my life in this city of 7 million people.

Over the days that followed I heard talk from my ministry leaders of the possibility of a team coming back to Chicago full time. I finally resolved with the Lord that if He wanted me to come back and join that team, I would. There ended up not being a team formed and I felt led to join a ministry team that traveled the next four years in the U.S. and around the globe. I met my wife during that time and ministered in dozens of countries. Both of us wanted to spend the rest of our lives in some foreign land sharing the gospel with those who had never heard. When the team decided to disband, my wife and I sought the Lord about where He would have us go next. I anticipated God sending us to work long-term with one of the tribal groups we had fallen in love with in Africa; or perhaps back to Asia to work with the struggling church there. We decided to pray separately and not tell each other what the Lord was speaking to us for two weeks. Then we could see if we were receiving the same direction. As you probably guessed, we both heard the Lord speak to us separately to form a mission team and return to Chicago long-term.

When we finally did share this with each other, we were both surprised. Once again I felt that somehow God was trapping me. Why would He ask us to work in a city when we had such a heart to reach the unreached nations of the world? Surely "urban ministry" was for a select few. I was a country boy. I couldn't relate to city culture. What was so important about the city? At that time, in the late '80s, cities were primarily only a Western phenomenon.[14] I wanted to finish the Great Commission and serve what God was doing in the unreached nations of the world. Little did I know that the developing world was about to explode in its own urbanization at a far faster rate than we had experienced in the West.

We began to pray for His heart for Chicago and cities in general. Over the next year we formed a team, went through further training, and headed out to the big city. Living that adventure for the last twenty years, I have discovered that God does in fact live in the city; that there may actually be something about the city that has a capacity to reveal the nature and character of God in ways we have never fully seen before. Furthermore, I have become convinced that the urban phenomenon sweeping the globe may actually be a part of a much bigger plan that God is unfolding. You may be like I was and have very little identification or appreciation for cities. Or you may be like many in this first urban generation who are actually drawn to the city. At the very least we need to understand God's role and attitude toward this global migration to have a relevant voice as the church in this age. Yet, what if there is a greater purpose for the church in relation to urbanization than just tolerating it, or seeking to finish God's purposes in the nations somehow in spite of the city—a purpose that if embraced could give God's people the tools to fill the earth with His glory?

I invite you to search this question out with me in this book. Either this global urbanization is one of the greatest challenges facing the church or its greatest opportunity. Could the growth of the modern city actually fit into the story God is writing on the earth? Can God's people display something of His nature and character on the earth through the context of the modern megacity that could not have been done otherwise? I would suggest that what is needed is a generation who can speak passionately and prophetically toward the city. Unless the church can feel comfortable moving into and making its home with God in the city, we are not prepared for the twenty-first century. My hope is that this book will help you understand why urbanization may be happening, who God is in relation to the city, and the role that we can play as we follow Him there. If we are to be the first urban generation in history, may we be prepared to steward that distinction well.

PART 1
THE CITY, OUR HOME

For He was looking forward to the city with foundations, whose architect and builder is God.
—**HEBREWS** 11:10

Chapter 1
THE MISSIONARY GOD

Then the disciples went out and preached everywhere,
and the Lord worked with them and confirmed
his word by the signs that accompanied it.
—MARK 16:20

Will the theology of mission we develop be merely a theology
of mission in the city or a theology of mission for the city?
—HARVIE CONN[1]

IN ORDER TO understand the times in which we live, we need an accurate worldview of history and of God's involvement in the direction of the human story. One of the most fascinating revelations given to us in the Bible is that of a God who is passionately on a mission. Not only did God create the world and man with a clarified purpose, but He is also revealed in Scripture as the One who is most jealously and actively pursuing the unfolding and recovery of that plan. The church's mission is never portrayed in Scripture as a delegated responsibility but rather a calling to follow what God is actively doing in the world. When we hold this understanding, then our mission in this world is

11

fueled and directed by His mission and the plan that He is unfolding. I am confident that the enemy of our Lord is not intimidated by the good things we do, but rather by those things we do in cooperation with what the all-powerful Creator of the universe is already actively working towards.

In the Psalms, David sings of the Lord's "thoughts" or "plans" that cannot be counted (Ps. 40:5; 92:5). This same Hebrew word is used by the Lord in Jeremiah when God speaks to the Israelites about knowing the plans He has for them (Jer. 29:11). The word literally means a "contrivance or machine, cunning, curious work and imagination."[2] The idea is that God has a thought-out imaginative contrivance that He is unfolding for the nations, as well as for you and me. God is unfolding the plan woven through history to buy back His original design for man. It's that plan that defines us, interprets history, and directs our activities as His followers into the future. What grand vision then is God working towards?

The book of Revelation is important for many reasons but perhaps most importantly because it reminds us of what God is moving history toward, and ultimately what He is returning His creation to. In Revelation 5, the apostle John is given a glimpse into an incredibly significant event in heaven. He realizes that in order for the human story to come to its closure, releasing the activity of God that will once and for all bring all things back into His original design, someone must be found who can open the scroll of the End Times. The question is raised in heaven by a mighty angel as to who is worthy to open the scroll. But no one in heaven or on Earth could open it. John begins to weep bitterly. Imagine the despair to discover that no one could bring about the end of the suffering of the universe;

that all hope is lost. However, one of the elders of heaven stops John and tells him not to weep because the Lamb of God had been found worthy to open the scroll.

What unfolds is an incredible celebration in heaven that is impossible to capture in words. A song begins to resound of the worthiness of Jesus because of what He had accomplished. By His blood He had purchased back for God men from every nation, language, tribe, and people. Furthermore He had bought back their destiny by making these nations, tribes, peoples, and languages a kingdom and priests to serve God and rule in the earth. In response to this declaration, heaven erupts with celebration and praise. Thousands upon thousands of angels begin to proclaim that Jesus is worthy to receive all honor and praise and glory for what He has accomplished. Following this, there erupts a resounding "Amen" from every creature in heaven and on Earth.

It is this glimpse into the future that reveals to us the completion of all that God has been working towards throughout history. Therefore, we can be confident that it is this goal that fuels and directs every activity of the Lord in every generation including our own. What is revealed in this scripture is something that God has accomplished in past tense (Rev. 5:10). What is being celebrated is something that God has done on Earth that is both ushering in the end of all things, and the beginning of the new. Two things are seen as marking the culmination of God's work throughout history: first, the buying back of mankind for relationship with the Father from all the expressions of diversity in the human story; and second, the reclaiming of their intended design to live out that diversity in a kingdom expression and service to God. It is this understanding of what God will one day ultimately celebrate that defines what He, and therefore we, are working toward reclaiming in some way today.

An Active God

In order to have an accurate worldview of history, we must start with the understanding that God is intimately and actively involved in the human story. He is not a passive God, simply watching history unfold with the nervous hope that all will not be lost. Rather, He is portrayed in Scripture as jealously fighting for and actively releasing His purposes on earth. This is, after all, His creation. It was His vision that brought forth the universe and the creation of a people made in His image. He is not only a Creator with infinite imagination and vision, but also a loving God who is committed to bring about the fulfillment of His loving vision for all that He created. He stands the most to lose relationally and has the capacity to experience the greatest grief over the disruption of those plans. (See Genesis 6:5–6.)

We must have a revelation that, more than any other, it is God who is most passionate about His creation. Because He is the most intelligent being in the universe, it is He who knows how to move history toward His desired end. Since He is all-powerful, having the capacity to accomplish all that He envisions, we are never more effective as His followers than when we are able to discern what He is doing and center all our activities on that plan.

The Scripture tells us that at the "fullness of time," Christ came (Gal. 4:4, nkjv). Wisdom was in operation, orchestrating certain events throughout history, to bring Christ at the appointed time. The same wisdom that brought Jesus to the cross, initiating the redemption of man, continues now before us to effectively reach the nations and reclaim all that He died for. This is what makes our mission, as His followers on the earth, an exciting adventure of intimacy with God. It's also what ensures our effectiveness! We are not left with some delegated or detached responsibility, seeking to fulfill a plan at which we are ultimately not powerful enough to succeed. Our effectiveness in completing the Great Commission will be to the degree that we understand God's investment in this world and draw upon it for His purposes.

Paul gives us a glimpse into the activity of God throughout history in Acts 17:26–27. Speaking to those in Athens, He declares that it is God who has made all the nations of men. In other words, the diversity of the human story was His idea and therefore has a purpose that He is committed to reclaim. He goes on to say that it is God who determines the exact places and times in which these nations should live. Throughout history God has been involved in when and where nations developed. He is even involved in where the nations of the world find their habitations. I do not believe this means that God is behind all the evils that destroy or displace the nations of the world. I do believe, however, that we can conclude that He is involved and has an interest in where they end up. Paul tells us why He is involved in this way in verse 27. He tells us that God is determining where the nations of the world are positioned in hopes that those environments would cause them to seek for Him and find Him, "Though He is not far from any one of us."

God uses environments to push us toward finding Him and give us a capacity to see Him. The problem is not getting God near us, but getting mankind to see Him and call out to Him. A biblical worldview of history should cause us to raise our eyes at any mass migration of nations or peoples from one geographical location to another and ask the question, "Is God involved?" If that migration is creating a hunger for God and capacity to see Him, then the answer may be yes. As people who follow His lead, we must then embrace these possible strategies of God as our own, and find our calling and involvement in them.

OUR INVOLVEMENT

After starting with an understanding of God's involvement in history, we then need a biblical understanding concerning our involvement. Since history is a story that God is ultimately writing, we find our meaning, significance, and purpose in that story. The glory on our lives is revealed or lost in how we either allow our story to be written into His, or seek to write our own apart from Him. Our callings and destinies are for the times in which we live. In the stories of David's mighty men, there were the men of Issachar who "understood the times and knew what Israel should do" (1 Chron. 12:32). In the story of Queen Esther and God's deliverance for the children of Israel, Esther's cousin reminds her, "Who knows but that you have come to your royal position for such a time as this?" (Esther 4:14). In the book of Acts we read the testimony of David's life and how he "served God's purpose in his own generation" (Acts 13:36). The idea is that there are times or eras that should define and determine our activities; that we are individually born into those times and given unique giftings that find their purpose in that bigger story; and that there are purposes of God that are playing out "in our own generation" that we can serve effectively. The Greek word used in this verse for *generation* means time or age[3] and the Greek word for *own* means "one's own, private or separate."[4] By implication it means that David was remembered as serving his own unique separate purpose pertaining to his age or time. It was a worthy legacy.

The disciples knew that God was moving history toward a desired end. At one point when Jesus was making reference to the future, the disciples asked what the signs of His coming and the end of the age would be (Matt. 24:3). Jesus then reveals many things concerning the End Times. In verse 14, He reveals that the "gospel of the kingdom must be preached in the whole world as a testimony to all nations" before the end would come. He speaks about wars, persecutions, and trials of all kinds, and that no one would know the day or hour because it would come when we least expected. Then in chapter 25, still answering the disciples' question concerning the End Times, Jesus puts the focus on how the kingdom of God will operate during those times.

The kingdom of God is the way in which God governs and relates to all that He has created. It's the ways of God revealed in relationship to the affairs of man. It is what Jesus reminds us to pray would be released on Earth as it is in heaven (Matt. 6:10). There is a way that God does things. It is always consistent with His character, and when understood, can provide both an explanation of what God is actively doing and an expectation of what He desires to do in the future. When Jesus appeared to His followers after His resurrection, He spent forty days talking to them about the kingdom of God (Acts 1:3). These were the ones who were going to build on all that He had accomplished through the Cross. It was an understanding of the ways of God and what God was governing throughout history that Jesus spent all of His time discussing with them before ascending into heaven. Why was this so important? Our calling is not to take the baton from Jesus, so to speak, and finish the race He started, but rather to follow the path He is already running and cross the finish line with Him. God has not delegated His dreams and plans to us. He has invited and called us to follow Him in those dreams. Because our ultimate calling is intimacy with the Father's heart, He has designed us to carry and steward along with Him the purposes of His heart for all that He has created.

HOW THE KINGDOM OPERATES

Jesus uses three parables in Matthew 25 to reveal how God's kingdom would operate in the End Times. They reveal both the activity of God and the activities of His followers. These three parables help to give us a sense of where God is going, and how we should govern our activities and expectations in relation to what He is doing. The first parable reveals how God is moving the human story toward a wedding and the focus of our expectation is the coming of the bridegroom (see vv. 1–13). His followers are warned in this parable to remain vigilant in the wait and ensure that their lamps are supplied with the oil necessary to keep them burning during that waiting period. It would seem that the lesson of this parable is the endurance and validation of the servants in the kingdom of God. The last parable is about the return of the Son of man and the gathering of His prized possessions, which are the nations (see vv. 31–46). The emphasis is on what the harvest will be; on a God who made His home with the broken and suffering in the world; and on those who knew Him enough to care for the same. It would seem that the lesson of this parable is about how God will handle the harvest at the end of all things.

However, it's the second parable that speaks specifically to the relationship between the activity of God and the activity of the church in the End Times. If the first parable is a lesson on the endurance of the servants in the kingdom of God and the last parable is the handling of the harvest brought in by those servants, then I suggest that it is this parable that speaks of the handling of the mission and the key to its success. What has commonly been called the parable of the talents in Matthew 25:14–30, has often been a lesson on how we should be responsible for the personal talents and gifts that God has given us. When we take this parable into the context of Matthew 24 and 25, understanding it as a direct answer to the question posed by the disciples concerning the End Times, we perhaps have a much larger meaning. The principle of personal responsibility over our talents is a biblical one. Yet, I suggest that the meaning and purpose of this parable is much greater.

Jesus reminds us at the beginning of the story that this is again a picture of what the kingdom of God will be like in the End Times (see v. 14 in reference to v. 1). The parable is about a man going on a long journey who entrusts his property to his servants. He gives different amounts to each of his servants according to their "ability" and then leaves. "After a long time" the man returns to see what the servants have done with his possessions. Two of the servants have multiplied his possessions while the third hid the master's property in the ground. He seems to be afraid that the master would demand something that he was unable to produce, and gives it back to him upon his return. The first two servants are praised and offered not only further responsibility but also the reward of the master's happiness. The third, however, is severely rebuked and cast out as someone who had no concern for, or relationship with, the master.

Jesus chooses three parables to describe how God's kingdom would operate in the End Times. Why is this story so important? Why is there an emphasis on each servant being given different measures of the master's property? Why is the third servant so harshly treated when he did not squander or lose the possessions of his master? I want to suggest that the lesson and importance of this parable relates to the way that the master entrusts his property to his servants, his expectation of what the servants are to do with that property, and the strategy for their effectiveness in that goal. It would seem that the third servant is judged precisely because of his inability or unwillingness to accurately perceive the master's involvement in that plan.

May I suggest that this is a parable about the mission of the church and the way that God partners with His church in that mission until His return? These are parables about the End Times. The first is about how we should posture ourselves in expectation for His return. The second is about the mission and its effectiveness as we wait for His return, and the third is about how He will handle His harvest once He has returned. Take a closer look at this middle parable. The story of the three servants begins with the master going on a long journey. This is a picture of Jesus and His ascension into heaven. Jesus then entrusts to His servants His property. According to Scripture the inheritance of Jesus is the nations (Ps. 2:7–8). What He has bought with His blood and intends to gather as His possession at the end are the nations (Matt. 25:31–32; Rev. 5:9). And it is the discipling of those nations that represents the ministry He has entrusted to us (Matt. 28:19). This is a missiological parable because it is about multiplying that property. It's about increasing the harvest of the nations. Therefore, it is important for us to understand the lesson of how Jesus is seen entrusting His servants with the harvest and what allows for the success of its multiplication.

When the master gives his property to the servants, the story tells us that he gives to each "according to his ability." The Greek word used for *ability* is found 116 times in the New Testament. However, this is the only time it is translated "ability." The word in Greek is *dunamis* and actually means "miraculous power," and "by implication a miracle itself."[5] In other words the word has nothing to do with one's own natural ability. It is used in Scripture the other 115 times to represent supernatural ability or mighty power from God. The Greek word used for *his*, in the phrase "according to his ability," is the same word we looked at in reference to David serving God's purposes in "his own" generation. It means, "one's own, private or separate."[6]

There are two very important lessons to this missions parable. First, when the master entrusted his servants with his possessions, he did not give to them according to their own ability but according to a supernatural ability entrusted to them. The third servant's indictment against the master that he "harvests where he has not sown and gathers where he has not scattered seed" was false and merely revealed the servant's ignorance of his master's character and ways. Second, the master gave his possessions according to each servant's own, separate, supernatural miracle. This is a revelation of how Jesus was going to complete His mission on the earth. His servants are the church. Since the parable plays out over the time span of when Jesus leaves and when He returns, we are still in this parable. I would suggest that the emphasis of three distinct and different servants reveals different representations of the church throughout the ages. He has given to those separate generational representations of His church a different measure of stewarding the multiplication of the nations, based on their separate, distinct, supernatural power given from God for the time in which they live.

We can have the confidence that our effectiveness in the stewarding of the nations is based on God's ability and not our own. We do not have to draw upon our own resources to finish the task. Rather, we simply need to discern the supernatural miracles in operation in the times in which we live, given to us for our effectiveness. When we carry the responsibility of missions without the expectation of discovering what the Lord is doing in our time then we are no better than the third servant. By not looking for God's involvement, we foster the belief, whether consciously or not, that He is a God who demands a return while doing nothing to ensure its success. However, this simply is not true. We are not only called to carry God's redemptive agenda into the world but have the joyous expectation of His involvement with us. This expectation will cause us to look at what is going on in the world around us and ask questions about the Lord's involvement, and seek understanding of what His Spirit may be doing to equip the church toward the fulfillment of His purposes in the nations.

ASKING THE RIGHT QUESTIONS

The supernatural ability given to the servants in Jesus' parable was specifically for access to, and multiplication of, the nations. The servants were given a measure of the master's possessions according to their own "miracles," and the first and second servants are seen multiplying those possessions according to their "miracles" as well. If it is our supernatural ability, entrusted to us by God, which gives us access to the nations and equips us with the power to multiply His possession of the nations, then what is our "miracle"? What activity of God, operating in the times in which we live, has He already sown that gives us a proximity to the nations and ability to disciple the nations in a way that we could not do otherwise? I believe it is the glory and intimacy of the church with the Father in every generation to seek the answer to that question.

By asking certain questions about God's involvement in the times in which we live, we can perceive those "miracles" that are meant for our effectiveness. Is there anything unique to our time that gives us effective access to the nations? Is there something unique about our generation, gifting the church with an ability to fulfill God's mission of redeeming all nations, which generations before did not have? Often, there can be more than one "miracle" in operation. However, our effectiveness in this world is determined by the degree that we discern these investments for our success, and embrace with anointing and authority, as God's stewarding agents, that which He is writing throughout history.

I would like to suggest that the phenomenon of global urbanization that we are witnessing today is one of those generational miracles for the purpose of completing the Great Commission and the fulfillment of what God is redeeming in the human story. Does urbanization create an opportunity for world evangelism in ways that have never been seen before? Does urbanization create a unique access to the nations and ability to disciple those nations into their kingdom and priestly expressions, in ways we could not have done otherwise? Furthermore, does the city create a unique setting for the truth of the gospel, the redemption of the human story, and the glory of God to be displayed on the earth? If not, then we merely need to understand how to fulfill God's dream on the earth in spite of the phenomenon of urbanization. However, if it does somehow fulfill these questions, then the church is called to not only embrace urbanization but also rush in with the excitement of harnessing its potential, and co-laboring with God in redeeming its purpose.

Paul exhorted the church in Ephesus to remember that our confidence in the task is based on the partnership we have with God's activity in every generation. Ephesians 3:20–21 says, "Now to him who is able to do immeasurably more than all we ask or imagine, according to his power [dunamis] that is at work within us, to him be glory in the church and in Christ Jesus throughout all generations [genea—times or ages], for ever and ever! Amen." Can we lift our eyes at the greatest urban migration in human history and see not only its potential for world missions but also a God who finds His home in the uniqueness of that environment? Who knows but that you were brought to existence for such a time as this? There are many stories being written on the earth. However, it is God's story that is most worth reading.

Chapter 2
THE FALLEN CITY

And when he drew near and saw the city, he wept over it.
—LUKE 19:41, ESV

God planned cities. We can know with certainty
that He wanted us to gather in city-communities
because He created us for togetherness.
—FLOYD MCCLUNG[1]

A N HONEST LOOK at cities would seem to challenge everything that I proposed about urbanization in the last chapter. There is a reason why *National Geographic* calls urbanization one of the four major challenges of our generation. The growth of cities worldwide has brought with it expressions of every form of brokenness, injustice, and cruelty in humanity. With 1.6 million people moving into cities every week come extreme poverty, racial and ethnic conflict, violence, and poor health conditions. According to *National Geographic*, most residents of third world cities lack sanitary sewage disposal, and about half have no adequate supply of drinking water.[2] Cities in Brazil are home to tens of thousands of street children, orphaned and living in extreme poverty. In the Philippines you can find whole communities living on garbage dumps. Cities throughout Asia are notorious for human trafficking and elaborate sex trades. The truth is that the average urban dweller lives with a daily reminder of man's brokenness and perversion.

I live in a city that has one of the highest murder rates in the nation, with 448 homicides recorded in 2010.[3] The public schools are outfitted with metal detectors and often kids are afraid to walk to and from school alone in fear of gang violence. Our first housing in Chicago was in a fifty-unit apartment building. Nearly every night you could hear domestic violence going on in one of the apartments down the hall. Sometimes it would seem to get out of hand and we would have to call the police. I asked a police officer, who came out one evening to our building, how the night was going. He looked at me with an exasperated expression. He said that easily two-thirds of their calls each night were to break up some domestic fight. Children growing up in cities are exposed to daily violence whether in their own homes, schools, or neighborhoods.

Every year we have dozens of mission teams who come and work with us in Chicago. During their orientation, I often ask them to list different things that come to mind when they think of cities. For twenty years now I have been asking that question. The answers are almost always the same. They quickly cite things like violence, gangs, drugs, prostitution, homelessness, poverty, tension, fast-paced life, over-crowdedness, and fear. What images come to your mind when you think of cities? Perhaps you see images of prostitutes and drug addicts on street corners, or inner-city kids living in poor housing projects. Maybe you think of crowded business districts where people seem rude and only concerned with their own needs.

All of these images beg the question: If the city is God's idea, why is there so much sin, violence, and human brokenness produced by urbanization? Many have argued that the existence of so much rebellion, pride, violence, and injustice is reason to believe that the city is man's idea, or at least the result of the devil's influence. However, I would suggest that we are drawing the wrong conclusion. Is there sin in the city? Yes. Does it seem there are many influences of darkness, perversion, and deception in the city? Without a doubt! The true question, however, is why.

MADE FOR RELATIONSHIP

The worldview of Scripture and the examples of history show that when men try to live together without the governing influence of righteousness, it produces evil. Men governed by selfish interest, fear, and self-protection, forced to live in close relation to others bent on the same, will not lead to harmony but chaos. However, it is not the idea of mankind living in relationship that is the problem; it's trying to succeed in that goal outside of our design.

God is a relater by nature. We, being made in the image of God, were fashioned for relationships. All of God's character traits are revealed in Scripture by how He relates. Even within the Trinity we have the example of God's relational character throughout eternity. We are never more displaying the image of God than when we are operating within relationships that would match His character. Likewise, our fallen state from that glory is never more evident than when it is displayed through the brokenness of our relationships. I would even argue that without the context for relationship we couldn't fully experience the redemption of that image.

The city, by its basic definition, is a group of people living, relating, and creating together in close geographical proximity. There is nothing contrary to the character of God or His design for man that wars against the basic concept of a city. As we will discuss a little later, Scripture actually reveals that the redemption of man is moving toward an increasing level of interrelating and relational proximity, not away from it. The Bible teaches that the man who isolates himself seeks his own desires (Prov. 18:1, ESV). It is the moving away from isolation into greater levels of interaction with others that defines our maturity. God finds His home in the city ultimately because He is the author of relationship.

Perhaps the problem is how big the city is. However, this argument would assume that there is a limit on how much relationship is healthy. Is there a point at which God is uncomfortable with how much relating is going on? Is there a point at which God can no longer provide what is needed for loving and productive interaction among mass amounts of people? Where do we put the limit? Is it at one million or five? How much relating is too much for God to handle? I would suggest that the greater the possibility for interrelating on every level—generationally, economically, and ethnically—the greater the possibility for God to be seen through the redemption of His image in us. The city is God's playground, not the devil's. The city intimidates the enemy precisely because it has the capacity to display the character of God in ways that define mankind and attract the hope of the nations to their purpose and design.

It could be argued that it is the very existence of so much evil and destruction in the city that shouts its importance. Jesus reminded us that He came to give life (John 10:10). This is the activity of a Creator, starting with nothing and bringing something into existence. In the same verse Jesus tells us that the enemy has come to steal, kill, and destroy. This is the activity of a Reactor. You cannot steal something that doesn't already exist, and you don't usually waste your time stealing something that doesn't have value. You cannot kill something that has no life in it. And, you cannot destroy something that is not first whole and viable. If there is such evil and destruction in the city, then the question we should be asking is, what is so valuable about the city that the enemy is spending so much effort seeking to steal, kill, and destroy?

Does the city threaten the enemy? Has the enemy created stigmas of fear about the city precisely to ensure that the church, as God's redeeming agent, would remain separated from its potential? As developed Western nations were urbanizing in the later half of the twentieth century, the church as a whole was seen leaving the city. In the last four decades, all recognizable annual church growth in North America took place outside the cities, in predominately monoracial and upper-middle class communities. While at the same time, most population growth was taking place in cities, with millions of immigrants moving into the very neighborhoods we were leaving. The city is a place of relational opportunity. The kingdom of God can only be displayed in the context of relationships, and even more so when those relationships display diversity. If that kingdom is to be seen as home to all the diversity of the human story, then the emergence of the diverse megacity is precisely the environmental context that most provides an opportunity for the witness of that kingdom. While the humanistic and sociological minds of our age are working furiously to reverse urbanization, the church should be embracing it wholeheartedly as the very environment that we were designed and anointed to live in.

PROTECTING THE VISION

God has a vested interest in the life of the city. The vision to see the diversity of the human story interrelating through community and spheres of societal influence was God's vision for man. Corporate entities are a type of life. In a Western individualistic worldview this can be harder to see. However, though much of the world relates to corporate identities more easily than Western culture, we nevertheless do in fact exist in corporate identities on a daily level. We identify ourselves as a part of a family. That family has a shared name, creating a belonging of the individual parts to a greater whole. An identity then develops into a corporate personality through the interacting of its unique individual personalities. That family has a unique purpose, revealed through the way in which the individual gifts and talents of its parts are functioning synergistically. We even see in Scripture a common perspective of corporate destiny and calling on families, providing both the expectation and ability to bless God and His purposes throughout the streams of history.

As believers we understand the importance of the family unit. The unity of its relationships has a great impact on the development and health of its individual parts. The interrelating context of the family also reveals something of the nature and character of God. The uniqueness of roles, function, and shared sacrificial love reveal aspects of God, perhaps in a way that could not be seen otherwise. It's for these reasons that the church has always fought for and sought to protect the value of family.

What we see in the purpose and significance of family identities can be understood through increasing levels of corporate realities as well. When multiple families begin to relate to each other in community, similar outcomes occur. We see recognizable differences in one community's personality, functionality, and gifting over that of other communities. Often these distinct communities develop their own languages, accents, or dialects reflecting a corporate set of values and expression of their corporate personality. A city is in essence a multitude of interrelating community clusters, like individuals of a family, acting out a corporate set of values, functionality, and unique personality.

Like the example of the individual family, cities likewise have a unique name expressing their origin, heritage, and sometimes purpose. The city is a unique expression of life different from other cities. Furthermore the city, with its synergistic functionality, has the capacity to bless other corporate entities. John Dawson, in his book *Taking Our Cities for God*, does a great job portraying the significance of corporate identity and purpose. He states that "a city is a human institution, and like all institutions it develops a creature hood or personality that is greater than the sum of its parts. Each metropolis has unique characteristics when compared with other cities."[4] I would argue that this reality exists because the city is, in fact, a type of human life.

Like the family, the church, more than any other group,

ought to understand the value of fighting for and protecting the city. God is the author of these types of corporate life. The existence of corporate life has existed for all of eternity within the Trinitarian expression of the Godhead. It could be argued that unless a type of corporate life, one that could be entered into by all the diversity of humanity, is created on earth, there will not be an adequate expression of the image of God in man. The city, with all of its potential for diversity and unity in relational expressions of shared life and loving sacrifice, then becomes a part of God's dream of making man in His image. It's something worth fighting for. There are many examples in Scripture where God speaks over these corporate expressions of life with singular calling, desire, and purpose, often holding them accountable to those directives in a corporate way. (See Jonah 4:11; Luke 13:34; Matthew 11:20–23.)

Scripture reveals a God who is looking for someone who will build a wall of protection around and fight for His vision for community (Ezek. 22:29–31). What bothered the Lord in this passage was that the people in that land practiced extortion, committed robbery, oppressed the poor and needy, and had mistreated the immigrant without justice. This sounds like the descriptions we attribute to the modern city. However, rather than wanting to judge, God is seen looking for a reason to protect His original vision for that corporate entity. It is God who understands what is most to lose in the loss of the city. He is working throughout history to protect and reclaim His original intent for man to carry the image of God. Because of the diverse interrelating of the city, the potential loss of that image is even greater than the individualistic expression of its parts.

RESTORING THE DREAM

An amazing picture of God's heart for the city is given to us in Ezekiel 36:33–38. He actually declares that the end result of His removing the people's sin would be a restoration of their cities and habitation in them. Their cities would be rebuilt, become productive and bear a harvest, and be protected once again. He even associates these restored cities as becoming "like the Garden of Eden." How could that be? Is it possible that the fellowship that man had with the Father in the Garden of Eden could take place in a city? The nations passed by and declared that these cities were like the Garden of Eden. The restored city had become a witness of God's original design, attracting the attention of those from the outside. I believe this is a picture of what God not only longs to do in our cities but also is actively fighting for. God declares that these restored cities would be both inhabited and fortified. His people would be attracted to and find their home in the city. The city would once again have a wall around it, protecting and fighting for the value that was within.

God declares, in reference to this vision of restored cities, that He had spoken, and He would do it (v. 36). In other words, it was His agenda and He was committed to bring it about. It was to become a witness to the nations of His power and restored blessing. It was even a sign of blessing to have these cities "filled with flocks of people" (v. 38, ESV). The city is not intrinsically evil. It could be seen as one of God's original designs for the expression of His image in man. I would argue that the enemy is working feverishly to distract God's children from the potential of the city; that he seeks to destroy the very image of God expressed through its interrelating of diversity with shared life and loving sacrifice; and he continues to generate an attitude of fear and intimidation to keep God's children from reclaiming the glory that is theirs in the city.

The reality is that evil, destruction, perversion, and brokenness exist in the urban world because those who have the capacity to bring light and truth have yet to make their home with God in that environment (Matt. 5:13). God deserves the right to be seen as both the author of relationships and the One with the greatest vision and purpose for the ever-increasing levels of diverse interrelating in the human story. We must conclude that whatever exists in the world with the greatest levels of interrelating generationally, ethnically, economically, and functionally, must be seen as where God resides. Furthermore, it is what God calls home that defines us as His followers, as well as that which He is ultimately moving the redeemed human story towards.

Do the modern megacity and the rate at which the world is urbanizing reveal incredible difficulties and brokenness? Yes. However, the idea of a city does not create these difficulties. Rather, it is the attempt at such complex interrelating, without the grace and direction of the One who is the author of those relationships, that produces the evils and suffering found in the city. The human story must by necessity move towards ever-increasing levels of diverse communities in order to discover the redemption of God's image in man. The prospect of increased urbanization without the direction of God and presence of His character-bearing people is hopeless and warranting of despair. Yet, if we fight for the city and its redeemed purpose, if we partner with God and apply a witness of His image in that context, it can become a hope to the nations and perhaps a discovery of the very design He has created us for. Later, we will look at examples of how the application of the image of God in diverse and complex relational community can truly display God's glory and draw the nations.

Chapter 3
LOOKING FOR HOME

*He led them by a straight way till they
reached a city to dwell in.*
—Psalms 107:7, esv

*The purpose of developing an urban theology is
not just to respond to the pessimism and ant-
urban prejudice found among most Christians,
but to help us respond obediently to God.*
—Floyd McClung[1]

THE SCRIPTURES TELL us that while wondering in
tents, Abraham by faith was looking forward to a city
with foundations, whose architect and builder was
God (Heb. 11:10) The Greek word for *city* in this scripture is
polis.[2] It's where we derive the term *metropolis*. Abraham
was looking for a city to call home. The phrase *looking
forward* literally means, "to accept from some source, to
await, expect, and look for."[3] Is there something about the
city that is meant to define us, causing an expectation in our
faith? Why would God be building a city and why would
He put that expectation in Abraham? Could our habitation

in a city be a part of our design and the reward that we should expect through His redemption of man?

Many struggle with the idea that cities could be in some way the unfolding of God's original purpose for man. After all, we started in a garden. Furthermore, one of the first mentions of man building a city in the Bible is seen invoking God's judgment (Gen. 11:1–9). In the twenty years that I have worked in Chicago, I continue to find the historical account of the Tower of Babel a struggle for many believers as they seek to understand the city. The traditional conclusion is that the city is the result of man's pride and self-exaltation; that God may have been upset with the building of cities in general. However, a closer look at the context and dialogue in this passage shows that it may have nothing to do with the idea of cities, but rather a specific act of rebellion toward the mandate God had given man in that age. Unless we see the city as a part of God's purpose for the human story, we will struggle to find the faith needed to embrace it and understand the role it plays in the reclaiming of our original design.

The first command that God gave to Adam and Eve was to be fruitful, multiply, and fill the earth (Gen. 1:28, ESV). After the Flood, when God chose to pass on the human story through Noah and his family, the first command given again is to be fruitful, increase in number, and fill the earth (Gen. 9:1). Then in Genesis 11 as men were moving eastward, still speaking the same language, they decided to settle in Shinar and build a city. They said to each other, "Come let's build ourselves a city, with a tower that reaches to the heavens, so that we may…[not] be scattered over the face of the whole earth" (Gen. 11:4). God looks down on this and decides to intervene. What is it that concerns the

Lord? God declares that, with one mind and one language, there was nothing impossible for them. So God confuses their languages. The result? Verse 8 declares, "So the LORD scattered them from there over all the earth." Then again in verse 9 we read, it was there that God confused the language of mankind, and "from there the LORD scattered them over the face of the whole earth."

The building of the city of Babel was a specific rebellion towards God's mandate to be scattered over the whole earth. Men decided it would be better to remain together; God intervened and sped up the purpose of man to fill the earth by confusing their languages. I would argue that even the act of confusing their languages was connected to the intended effect of man filling the earth. God was moving the human story toward His original design in spite of man's resistance.

Acts 17:26 tells us it was God who created all the nations. It was His original goal that diversity would develop. Without diversity there could not be the possibility of an expression of unity in that diversity as an adequate image of God in man. If men filled the earth as they had been commanded, diversity would have developed naturally. Culture and language derive and develop through isolation and geography. The culture and language that would develop in people of the Himalayas would be vastly different from those in the desert plains of Africa. Likewise, the peoples of landlocked cold climates would develop differently than those of island nations. This was God's plan. It was precisely the rebellion toward this plan that God judged and corrected in the account of the Tower of Babel.

Some have argued that it was the desire of men to make a name for themselves that prompted the building of a city; that cities are nothing more than an attempt at self-glorification. However, it would seem that the problem was not in making a city but in trying to make a name for themselves different than the name God wanted written on the earth at that time. It wasn't the time for settling and building, but scattering and filling. It was the epoch of human history centered on the building of diversity. Once the nations had been developed the way God had planned, we then would be able to enter the epoch of history in which the diversity of the world could begin to relate to each other in expressions of unity and Christlike love, revealing the redeemed image of God on the earth. It is this epoch of human history that I suggest we are seeing unfold in our time.

Though we started in a garden, we were never meant to stay there. This was the infancy of the human story. Even before the Fall, the command was given to fill the earth. God is still working toward His original plan for man in spite of the entrance of sin into the world. It is to the glory of God's children to understand that plan and work towards it. We were created to develop into ever-increasing levels of relationship, creating on the earth not only individual expressions of life but corporate expressions of life as well. As men filled the earth and the nations developed, cities were naturally built. We were made for community, and history is full of these expressions of complex inter-relating. Much of that history reflects man's attempt at community and corporate life apart from God and the standards of His character. However, cities do not intimidate or war against God's plan for man, but rather help to complete it. The city whose architect is God is a part of our redemption. As we will see later, Scripture reveals that God actually chooses to put His name, that which describes His character, on the idea of a city.

HOME SWEET HOME

We may be surprised to find that the Bible actually defines our future home (heaven) as a city. As I mentioned earlier, the book of Revelation is meant to give us a glimpse into what God is redeeming and moving history towards. The culmination of God's redeeming story on the earth is found in the last two chapters of the Bible. While man was created in a garden in the first chapter of Genesis, he is found entering the context of a city as his eternal home at the culmination and redemption of all things. In the vision given to John, he sees a new heaven and new Earth after the old had passed away. He then sees a Holy City, the New Jerusalem, coming out of heaven "prepared as a bride beautifully dressed for her husband" (Rev. 21:2). A loud voice is heard from the very throne of God, declaring, "[Now] the dwelling place of God is with man" (v. 3, ESV).

The city is equated with the bride of the Lamb. It's a corporate entity that is now revealed as a single unified bride. Since all those who have accepted the Lord are a part of that bride, then all believers are seen in John's vision as being involved in a corporate life called the New Jerusalem. Not only will we live in the most complex multiethnic city ever fashioned, but God also declares that His home will forever be in relationship with this corporate entity called a city. The bride and the city are one, "beautifully dressed for her husband." As if to further clarify the significance of this picture, John is again taken to a high mountain to see "the bride" and is shown the "Holy City, Jerusalem" (vv. 9–10). How is it that the city has become that which defines our eternal home? If the city is our eternal home then it has been our design from the beginning, since God only redeems what He Himself has purposed.

Lest we think this picture is simply a metaphor, John's revelation includes the angel actually measuring out the city, describing its gates, streets, and activities. The city is measured as approximately 1,400 miles wide, 1,400 miles long, and 1,400 miles high. The dimensions of this city will span nearly one-third the landmass of the U.S. It's a city that will cause the agglomeration of Tokyo's thirty-seven million people and all earthly projections at growing cities to pale in comparison. Its size as a single city is nearly unimaginable. It will house every nation, language, tribe, and people in such relational unity that they function as one bride. No longer will there be a temple where we go to meet with God, since He will relationally dwell there. There will be no need for a sun or moon because the glory of God's presence will literally fill the city.

This is the fulfillment of the human story. Our home will forever be the complex interrelating of a city. We will live and find our meaning in the most complex, diverse expression of community the world has ever imagined. It's a city built by God. His throne will be there and He will govern this kingdom expression called a city with loving intimacy for all of eternity. When Adam and Eve brought sin into the world they were cast out of the Garden lest they should eat of the tree of life, and secure a corrupted and fallen form of existence different than what God had intended. An angel was sent to guard the tree of life so no man could eat of it and create some eternal life apart from the purpose that God had envisioned for man. Yet now we see in John's revelation that the tree of life has been restored to man and it is found on the main street of the New Jerusalem (22:2).

The Garden and the city have now become one. Its leaves are for the healing of the very nations that God Himself created. The bookends of man's story have now been brought together. God has done it. He has reclaimed His original intent for mankind. In spite of our fallen struggle, He has created the diverse expression of His image in man, and redeemed the purpose and glory of that diversity through purifying and unifying it into a single bride. And He has given that bride, as a wedding gift, a home envisioned, fashioned, and built by His own hands, called a city.

MANSIONS IN THE SKY

Can we consider seriously for a moment the home that we are looking forward to eternally? When you picture heaven, what do you think of? When you envision the home that Jesus is preparing for you, what does that look like spatially and in relationship to the home He is making for others at the same time? If we are honest, most of our traditional descriptions are pictures of isolation or at least controlled exposure to others. Whenever we are dealing with difficult relationships, we tell ourselves that we can't wait to get to heaven where we will not have to deal with people anymore. We endure community when it is imposed on us but are looking forward to the day when we can graduate from that crowded lifestyle and get "away from it all." We sometimes comfort ourselves that at least in heaven we will get peace and quiet. What picture comes to your mind when you think of peace, relaxation, and happiness? Does it involve a lot of people? For most people, their "happy place" is one away from others, where they can be uninterrupted. In other words, what we often seek as reward is isolation.

I would like to suggest that the reasons we seek isolation may have little to do with what we are actually being redeemed for, and more to do with a reminder of what still needs to be redeemed. Perhaps it's the fallen state of our humanity that frustrates our earthly attempts at community. It is the existence of selfishness, fear, and self-protection that causes us to repel from relationships. Isolation is not our reward but the exposure of our brokenness. A sign of our maturity and redemption is our ability to not only tolerate complex interrelating but to actually be attracted to it. Yet we do not expect this if the reward we expect in heaven is a picture of solitude and the chance to finally get away from others.

In John's Gospel we find a passage where Jesus is encouraging His followers about heaven. They are told to not lose heart, though He is about to leave them, since He is going away to prepare a place for them. He further encourages them that He will assuredly return to take them there so they can be where He is (John 14:1–2). This is a picture of a bridegroom, who after He has entered into the engagement covenant, goes away to prepare the home for His bride. What exactly is this home that Jesus is preparing? Jesus creates an interesting picture of heaven in this passage, which is meant to give us an understanding of our design and the hope of its return.

In the King James Version, John 14:2 is translated: "In my Father's house are many mansions: if it were not so, I would have told you. I go to prepare a place for you." This has been a favorite passage of hope and expectation for many waiting for their eternal home. However, what exactly is the picture that Jesus is painting for us in this promise? A deeper look at the words Jesus chose in this scripture may give us a definition of our eternal home that we are missing. The Greek word used for the Father's house is *oikia*, which means place of residence, abode, and by implication, family.[4] The first picture Jesus gives us is that our eternal home is in fact a part of a family. We have been given a home in God's family and personal place of residence.

The definition of heaven, therefore, is a place of belonging to a larger community that God Himself identifies with and resides in. We will live in God's house as a part of His family and in relationship with all of His children. Next, we are told that it is in that place that the Father has waiting for us what the King James Version of Scripture calls "mansions." The Greek word translated here as mansion is used only two times in the New Testament. The word is *mone*, which actually means "a staying."[5] It's the act or place of residence. The other time it is used is in John 14:23 (KJV), in which Jesus promises to those who love Him that He and the Father would come and make their abode (*mone*) with them. The verb form of this word is *meno* and is used 105 times in the New Testament. It means, "to stay, abide, continue, dwell, and endure."[6] In other words, the promise is that the place in the Father's house that Jesus will prepare for us is a place of staying, enduring, and continuing. It's a place of eternal abiding and remaining, one that we will never have to leave.

Jesus gives us an amazing picture of belonging in the Father's family and the enduring permanence of that home. He then promises to go and prepare a place for us. The Greek word used here for place is *topos*. It is one of two words used commonly in the New Testament to describe location. This word actually means "a spot, limited by occupancy."[7] It is contrasted with the Greek word *chora*, used twenty-seven times in the New Testament, which has a more expansive meaning such as territory, coast, country, land, or region.[8] Yet Jesus did not use this word; instead, He chose the word that describes a spot, limited by occupancy. When we break down this passage we get a beautiful picture of what Jesus is preparing for us. The promise that Jesus gives is one of belonging in a family and having an assured spot in that family prepared for us that will endure forever. It's a picture of community. Jesus doesn't say, "In the Father's abode are many lands, islands, territories, and regions and yea, you will have your own, far from anyone else." Why then do we picture a form of isolation, with perhaps only a few of our most trusted earthly relationships, as the home that Jesus is preparing for us?

Like the revelation given to John in the New Jerusalem, this passage reminds us that we are being prepared for community. Our very design is marked for relationship and it is the context of diverse relational proximity that we are being redeemed for. Every believer who has existed in the past, those existing today, and all who will believe on Jesus in future generations will have their home in the New Jerusalem. Even by conservative projections, if we consider the number of Christians on the earth today, along with those of every century before, added to the possible harvest of just one more century, the number of believers in that city could be equal to the entire population of the globe today. I am, of course, suggesting a hypothetical possibility to describe the density of population in the New Jerusalem. Yet, if these projections were true, what would it be like to have the population of the entire globe today, over six billion people, living in a landmass one-third the size of the United States? Though these figures may be impossible to accurately project, without a doubt, the picture portrayed to us in Scripture is one of intense community.

A Fit for All Personalities

Normally, when I share this particular view of heaven with groups, I see worried looks on some of the faces. There are those among us who have the personality type that thrives on being around people, and then there are those who enjoy being alone and sometimes need it to refuel. I know because I am one of them. I am naturally a quiet person. I can enjoy sitting by myself reading a book for hours. And like most introverts, I refuel and get energized by that alone time. It's important for us to understand that the home that Jesus is creating for us will fit us all. Being either an extrovert or an introvert is just a part of the unique way that our loving Father has made each of us. However, in our current state there is a fallen aspect to all of our personality types.

We were all made for relationships. As we grow and mature into the likeness of Christ, we will appreciate those relationships more and more and find our home in them. This is a sign of maturity. For an introvert that maturity may be the ability to function more productively in relationships; for the extrovert it may mean the ability to function relationally with more other-centeredness. To the introvert, God may be working to remove the fear and stress that has crept into her relational design, while relational maturity for the extrovert could be the freedom that is gained when his wholeness is so secure in Christ that he can now enjoy relationships without the need to meet some inner deficit.

In the New Jerusalem we will see redemption expressed in both God's original relational design for us, and also in the unique personality differences that He has created in us for His enjoyment. The full design of who God intended us to be will find its complete fulfillment in this city. After John relays this magnificent defining vision of our eternal home, he goes on to say in Revelation 21:25 that the gates of the city will never be shut. We do not have to worry about being confined to the city. We will forever explore and reign with Christ over the entire universe. Who knows but that you may have a planet that is a secret place for just you and Jesus to dwell in together? The city will be a place of coming and going. It will be a place of activity. However, though each of us may express our unique personalities and desires throughout God's universe, two defining realities will forever exist. First, it is the city that every nation, language, tribe, and people will call home. And second, it is to that unified, loving, corporate identity that God will forever dwell with and marry Himself.

What picture do we paint for people when we talk of heaven and our eternal home? Does our picture match what God has created us for and is jealously fighting to reclaim? If our picture of what we are being prepared for is different than God's, then we will not have eyes to see where He is going. Furthermore, if the picture of our redemption is different than God's, it is a lesser glory and one that will not attract the nations or speak adequately to the longing of men's hearts. Are we, like Abraham, looking forward to a city whose architect is God? If the city is to be our eternal home, how does God prepare us for that existence? If God's kingdom is to be displayed as a witness to all nations before Jesus returns (Matt. 24:14), then how do we most adequately display a witness of the kingdom we are all being prepared for? If it's a city built by God that the nations are being prepared to enter for all eternity, then it's to the cities that God's children must go today, in order to ignite those nations with an appetite for home.

Chapter 4
GETTING CLOSE TO GOD

I will get up now and go about the city, through its streets and squares; I will search for the one my heart loves.
—SONG OF SOLOMON 3:2

Its one thing to have God's strategy for the city, but it's another thing to have God's presence within the people attempting to minister.
—JOHN DAWSON[1]

I F YOU COULD go anywhere and spend some quality time with your heavenly Father, where would you go? I love the mountains. I think the perfect time with the Father would be sitting next to a warm fire, sipping a strong cup of coffee, while looking out the window at majestic snowcapped mountains. I always dreamed of working somewhere in a small mountain community where I could return home every night to a peaceful, secluded cabin. I would have a trail marked out that would lead down to a bubbling mountain stream on the edge of our property. It would be equipped with a bench sitting next to the edge of the stream where I could talk to God in the midst of chirping birds and small animals rustling in the brush. It was my perfect picture of getting close to God (I told you I'm an introvert). So why did God ask me to spend my life working in a city with millions of people?

When I answered God's call on my life to be a missionary, I was prepared to go to jungles, isolated mountain villages, and even arid deserts. I was ready to spend the rest of my life in some prison behind the iron curtain trying to take the gospel to the unreached. I never thought I would be in a megacity, living in multiunit apartment buildings, and surrounded daily by masses of people. Our first apartment in Chicago was a small studio in a fifty-unit building. We were on the second floor, with the city's elevated subway train located outside our window. The train ran past our window every three to five minutes, twenty-four hours a day. It shook the apartment. People lived above us, below us, and on either side of us. The walls were not very thick so you could also hear the neighbors 24/7.

I grew up in small rural and suburban communities. I'm not sure if I had ever heard a police car run past our house with its sirens blaring as a boy. However, this was a daily occurrence around our apartment in Chicago. Not only did police cars race past us daily but also ambulances, narcotics cops, and fire trucks. Added to all this noise was the constant domestic squabbles and ruckus from the apartments down our hall. Since we lived on an alley, we could hear our neighborhood prostitutes, drug dealers, and street gangs making their rounds outside our window each night. As a young missionary setting out to follow God, I could not have entered a more foreign environment.

I had been serving God in missions for several years prior to this move. Yet I was unprepared for what the Lord had thrust me into. I loved my times with the Lord. My alone times with God had become not only a discipline but also a lifeline, and something I looked forward to each day. However, in the first few months of living in Chicago, I began to struggle in my intimacy with the Lord. I would sit to have my quiet times but would struggle with constant distraction. No matter what time of day I would schedule my times with God, there was always activity going on that hindered my focus. I would read Bible passages over and over, but not because of meditating on some deep meaning; I simply kept getting distracted by the trains, the noises on the street, or the voices in the apartments next to me. Even as I sought God's presence and practiced hearing His voice throughout my daily activities, my thoughts were always clouded and overloaded by the visual and audio stimuli going on around me. Just the atmosphere of a city can wear you out. Your spirit is constantly aware and sensitive to all the emotional and spiritual dynamics of the thousands of people you casually brush past on a moment-by-moment basis. I was drying up inside and feeling increasingly alienated form God's presence.

As teams would come to our city to work with us for different weeks throughout the year, I would hear the same comments. People would ask me how I could keep refueled in the Lord and get alone with God. They would say things like, "It must be hard to hear God in a place like this," and "Do you ever get a chance to get away and spend some time with God?" I understood these questions; they were the questions I was asking the Lord. People who considered coming to work with us in the city voiced the same concerns, saying things like, "I am just not sure I could hear

God in a place like this," or "I'm not sure my relationship with God is strong enough."

AN UNEXPECTED ANSWER

A few months into our new city life, I began to cry out to the Lord. I was looking for God to create some spot in the city where I could get alone with Him and hear Him clearly. I needed Him to recreate what I was accustomed to in my times alone with Him, namely privacy and quietness. I was surprised one day when I felt the Lord telling me to go to one of our busiest neighborhood streets to have my "quiet time." Devon Street is in the heart of our Indian and Pakistani district. This South Asian business district caters to the 300,000 South Asians living in our city. Scattered along the street are benches used by the men and women of the neighborhood who come out to talk and socialize. I chose one that was not being used at the time.

Because 75 percent of our taxi drivers in Chicago are Asian Indian or Arab, the street was packed with taxi drivers shopping at the Asian food markets and restaurants. The sidewalks were filled with people shopping from dozens of different language groups all dressed in their vibrant cultural clothing. People who walked by grabbed my attention with their unique dress, languages, and activity. I was a little surprised that the Lord would want me to go there to have my "quiet time" with Him. The sensory overload was enormous!

I began to read my Bible and try to listen to what the Lord wanted to say to me. Needless to say the experience was just as distracting, if not more so, as what I had been dealing with the previous few months. I struggled through my quiet time, and as I was preparing to leave, I sensed the

Lord telling me to return there again the next day. Surprised but willing, I returned, and returned, and returned, as I continued to hear God telling me to do so each day.

The first several days were difficult but then something began to happen. I realized that I had been looking at this wrong. I assumed that the only way to hear God was in private, and isolated from human activity. As I continued to come out to this busy street, two things began to happen. First, I began to train myself to focus on the Lord's voice in spite of all the voices going on around me. I was learning how to enter into a bubble of intimacy with the Lord while being surrounded by an overload of stimuli.

This was incredibly freeing. I was being intimately refueled with the Lord's presence in the midst of the masses of humanity. Even more surprising was what happened next. God began to speak to me intimately through the visual and relational stimuli going on around me. What had been a distraction previously was now being used by God to make His presence more known to me. The scriptures I was reading were becoming alive and relevant to what I was seeing at the moment. The Lord's character and activities were being discovered through observing the masses of diverse humanity that swarmed around me.

ENVIRONMENTAL PRESENCE

I began to discover that my struggle in sharing intimate times with the Lord in the context of a city had more to do with my previous orientation than with the limitations of my environment. Furthermore, it became clear that even what I considered a limitation could become an asset in experiencing God's presence. Do we believe that God is more likely to be found in nature than in a city? What does that communicate to an ever-increasing urban world that may never have the chance to leave a city and experience "nature"? This perspective can alienate God from an urban generation, creating the idea that the city is at odds with God and His habitation. Do we truly believe that those who live in environments surrounded by the beauty of mountains, forests, and waterfalls have an ability to interact with the presence of God more than those who do not?

We may find it hard to theologically agree to such a thought, but what do we portray in our actions and words? Are we unconsciously telling an urban world that if you really want to get close to God, you have to leave the city? Why do we speak of the majestic environment described earlier as "God's Country" while calling the city a place where God is distant and even perhaps absent? Is God waiting for us all to move to the country so we can be where He is? What would happen to the country if we did in fact all move there? Would God have to leave because it would no longer be the quiet secluded environment that He prefers? I am speaking facetiously, but much of our Christian language has, in fact, revealed this belief. Notwithstanding the implications this idea has on an urban world, how does it relate to the nations of the world who live in diverse forms of geography? Is the family who lives in the desert regions of the Sahara handicapped because they will never experience majestic forests and mountain streams? Are the tribal groups living on Pacific islands handicapped in their intimacy with God because they will never see the snowcapped Alps?

When we define our capacity to relate intimately with God in environmental terms, we have actually reduced God to an environment. We confuse those not from the environment of our own orientation and ultimately alienate God from much of the world. Even the concept of taking retreats or vacations to refuel is an economical privilege shared by a very small percentage of the world's population. Is God only the God of the middle and upper classes? Most of the world will never have the means to leave the environment that they grew up in. These are the practical dilemmas associated with such a thought, but are there theological complications to this perspective as well? If we were honest, many of us would admit feeling that we would somehow pollute the view of Scripture by saying that God's presence can be purely enjoyed in the city as much as in nature.

DISCOVERING GOD IN CREATION

Psalms 19 gives us a beautiful picture of the impact that God's creation has on the earth: "The heavens declare the glory of God; the skies proclaim the work of his hands" (v. 1). It goes on to say that there is no speech or language where their voice is not heard; "Their voice goes out into all the earth, their words to the ends of the world" (v. 4). The handiwork of the Lord in this passage are the heavens, the skies, and the sun. Every person on the earth sees them. There is no culture or nation that has escaped hearing the declaration of God's glory. What does this specific handiwork of the Lord reveal to us about God? For sure they reveal to us His creativity, His might, and order.

Perhaps the most well-known passage about seeing God's glory in creation comes from Romans 1:18–20. God actually says that all men are without excuse because His invisible qualities have been clearly seen by "the things that are made" (KJV). The Greek word here is *poiema*, and is only used twice in the New Testament. It means a "product or fabric, workmanship."[2] The only other time it is used is in Ephesians 2:10, which says, "We are God's workmanship (*poiema*), created in Christ Jesus to do good works." The two references to the glory of God being seen through His creation are in relation to the skies and the crown of His creation, man. These are the two aspects of His creation that all men are exposed to. There is nothing in these scriptures that convey the necessity or advantage of being near God's majestic landscapes and earthly creatures as a means of discovering Him. It could be argued that since we are the crown of His creation and that which is made in His image, we are possibly at a greater advantage of witnessing the glory of God and His invisible qualities when we are around people, not isolated from them. Furthermore since Christ is the image of the invisible God (Col. 1:15), and it was predestined that we as God's workmanship be in Christ (Eph. 2:10), we never bring God's presence upon the nations more than when Christ, in us, lives among them.

We cannot define our ability to experience God's presence and intimacy in either geographical terms or environmental standards. Surely our personalities, the orientation of our culture, and our upbringing can influence our preferences. However, we cannot limit God to those things. In doing so, we find ourselves limiting our ability to go anywhere that God leads and the confidence that we will find Him there when we arrive. God is where people are. As Revelation 21:3 reminds us, it is with people that God makes His dwelling. I love His creation and, as mentioned earlier, prefer majestic scenery and interaction, with the beauty He has woven into that creation. Yet, I am no longer handicapped in the city. I have found that God resides there. He lives among people and His presence can be felt as we walk among the masses. Furthermore, it is the beauty found in the complex diversity of those people that shouts to me most the glory of God. I may learn things of God's power, strength, and majesty in nature; but I have discovered His character, emotion, and presence among people. Even His power, strength, and majesty are never seen more than when they are applied to redeeming people. Remember that it was this display of God's handiwork that caused the heavens to erupt and sing of His worthiness (Rev. 5:9–10).

Over the last two years, I have had the privilege of helping to develop and lead urban-focused Discipleship Training Schools (DTS) in Youth With A Mission (YWAM). The goal of an urban-focused training school was to address the unique challenges that an urban generation is facing, and give them the tools to know God and make Him known in an urban world. YWAM has been training and mobilizing young people through its discipleship training schools worldwide for nearly fifty years. However, we began to realize that we needed to teach a new generation these tried and true principles of knowing God in an urban context lest they enter the urban world with the same struggles that I described earlier.

Students in DTS are taught how to develop their alone times with God and participate in scheduled daily "quiet times." In the Urban DTS, however, they are taken into busy and diverse parts of the city regularly to practice dwelling with God. They may be sitting on a street corner in the middle of a bustling business district, or in dirtier parts of town surrounded by homelessness and drug addicts, or perhaps surrounded by people from dozens of different cultures. I love watching the students as they struggle through this process. Each of them experiences that monumental breakthrough of discovering God's presence and hearing His voice in the midst of the city and the masses of its people.

Like me, most of the students set out with a level of disbelief in being able to hear God among so much distraction. Yet, an amazing thing happens when they discover God's presence in the city and the fulfillment of intimately interacting with Him there. An overwhelming confidence comes upon them. As if for the first time, they begin to feel that they could go anywhere, knowing that no environment can steal their ability to fellowship with God. Imagine if we had a generation who was able to transcend their cultural and geographical orientations and have the capacity to hear God and fellowship with His presence in any environment. This would be the most enduring and equipped-for-missions generation the world has ever seen.

ENVIRONMENTAL HOLINESS

A deeper struggle for some has been envisioning God, and therefore His people, dwelling with the corruption and sinfulness of the city. How can we have pure intimacy with God when all around us we see the ugliness of sin and perversion? How does God live in the city among so much rebellion, hatred, and selfish behavior? Can we live in the city and still be pure? Is our ability to fellowship with God's presence hindered because of the unwillingness in God's Spirit to dwell where sin is? I would suggest that this struggle is the result of a false understanding of God and His holiness.

Sin does not remove God's presence from us but removes our ability to see and fellowship with His presence. When we walk in sin, we are relationally alienated from the God who is there. When we harbor sin in our hearts, it causes a removal of fellowship, not a removal of God. Remember that Acts 17:27 reminds us that God is working to position the nations so that they will seek and reach out for Him, though He is not far from any one of us. Why have we made God the One who runs away instead of us? While we were yet sinners, Christ died for us (Rom. 5:8, KJV). When Adam and Eve rebelled against God, it was God who walked the Garden asking, "Where are you?" It was not man searching for God (Gen. 3:8–9). When Jesus came into the world, the verdict was not that the light couldn't stand the darkness but the darkness couldn't stand the light (John 3:19). The Scriptures reveal a God who strives with men even in their darkness. David declared, "Where can I flee from your presence?" and "Even...the darkness is as light to you"(Ps. 139:7–12).

God is not intimidated by sin. To be sure, He hates sin and we ought to as well (Prov. 8:13). Yet He is not a God who hides from sin but actively engages it with a jealous desire to eradicate it from the human story. God is a holy God. Yet His holiness is not derived from a geographical separation from sin, but a lack of sin in His being. God says of Himself in Isaiah 57:15, "This is what the high and lofty One says—he who lives forever, whose name is holy: 'I live in a high and holy place, but also with him who is contrite and lowly in spirit, to revive the spirit of the lowly and to revive the heart of the contrite.'" God Himself declares that He dwells, literally makes His lodging with,[3] those who are contrite and lowly in spirit.

Often the phrase *contrite and lowly in spirit* is interpreted as those who are repentant of heart. However, the meaning of this phrase in the passage above may be broader. The Hebrew word for *contrite* means crushed like powder, destruction.[4] The Hebrew word for *lowly* or *humble* means depressed.[5] The broader context of this scripture seems to be addressing those who have continually rebelled against God. Though they continue to resist Him, He has declared that He will not be angry forever. He has chosen to make His home with those who are crushed like powder and depressed in their spirits, that He might revive them. God is a God who dwells with brokenness. He is not far from any of us and longs to restore and redeem our broken lives. It is the kindness of the Lord that leads us to repentance, not our repentance that invokes His kindness (Rom. 2:4).

The brokenness of the world and the perversion of His image in man do not cause God to run away but rather ignite His jealous desire to redeem. It is actually His holiness that compels Him to dwell with us in our sin and not run away. It's precisely His holiness that translates into longsuffering over the sin of the world. Some have argued that the judgment on Sodom and Gomorrah displays God's unwillingness to put up with evil in a society. However, it is the account of Sodom and Gomorrah that reveals God's longsuffering and willingness to strive with men's wickedness as long as possible. God tells Abraham that He would be willing to spare these wicked cities if only ten righteous people could be found in them (Gen. 18:16–33). Like in Ezekiel 22:29–31, God is looking for someone who will stand in the gap and fight for the city so He will not have to destroy it. The lesson of Sodom and Gomorrah is not how much God hates wickedness, but how much confidence He has in His ability to change wickedness when His people dwell with Him in that place.

God's passionate hatred of sin is fueled not by the discomfort that sin may cause Him, as if His proximity to sin will somehow cause Him to feel dirty; the hatred God feels toward sin is in proportion to His commitment to what is right and loving. It is this commitment that compels Him to draw near and pursue those in sin that He might restore them. It is God's loving and redeeming nature that causes Him to make His home with the broken who are crushed and depressed in spirit. This is a sign of holiness, not impurity. Jesus, who is the exact representation of the Father (Col. 1:15), was criticized by the religious leaders of His day for His constant habit of being with sinners (Matt. 11:19). God, revealed in Christ, is seen dwelling in the midst of sinners. When the religious leaders confronted Jesus about His relentless habit of being with the sinners and outcasts, He simply tells them that He did not come for those who are well, but sick (Matt. 9:12).

Why do we insist that God's presence needs be in sterile environments, isolated from the filth of the world? Jesus did not stay in the synagogues. He walked the streets where prostitutes hung out. He had dinner with extortionists and those who lived in selfish and perverted lifestyles. He was compelled to do so because of His holiness. If God makes His home with the broken and sinful, then so must we. Why have we defined our holiness as isolation from the world? This kind of definition will cause the church to remove itself from the very ones that God desires to live among.

Jesus told His followers that His goal was not to take them out of the world but that they would remain protected from the world (John 17:15). Praying to the Father, He declares, "As you sent me into the world, I have sent them into the world. For them I sanctify myself, that they too may be truly sanctified" (John 17:18–19). Jesus reveals the key to our holiness: it's not our removal from the world, but rather our being sanctified by Him in the midst of the world. We are meant to be where God is. God dwells with the lost. Holiness for the believer is not a geographical reality but an internal one. The degree to which we are compelled to dwell among the lost, driven by a jealous desire to protect, reclaim, and restore people, is the degree to which we are actually experiencing the holiness of God.

By allowing ourselves to define holiness in terms of geographical proximity to sin, we are robbing the church of the identity it was meant to have. Worse still, we are unable to dwell where God is and impotent in our ability to reveal Him to a dying world. When we isolate ourselves from communities of brokenness out of a need to protect our purity we actually lessen the work of Christ, and misconstrue what is true purity. It is precisely the witness of our ability to live in the world and not be overcome by it that brings glory to God and hope to the nations. Unless we can redefine true holiness to the church in this urban generation they will not find the faith to live with God in the city. Unless we can train a generation, forced to live in the city, with an ability to intimately know God in the complexity of urban environments, we are simply not discipling the nations in the age in which we live.

PART 2
THE CITY, OUR GIFT

Lift up your eyes and look about you: All assemble and come to you; your sons come from afar, and your daughters are carried on the arm.
—Isaiah 60:4

Chapter 5

THE NATIONS ARE COMING

*Now there were staying in Jerusalem God-
fearing Jews from every nation under heaven.*

—ACTS 2:5

*Mission is no longer about crossing the oceans, jungles and
deserts, but about crossing the streets of the world's cities.*

—RAY BAKKE[1]

IN 1991, I was a part of an advance team of twenty-plus
missionary students who had traveled to Chicago for
two months to do ministry in the city. We also hoped to
"spy out the land" for our team preparing to move there six
months later. It was an eye-opening experience. During one
of our first evangelism times we were talking to people in
a large plaza downtown. After being there for only a short
time, a man in his late thirties walked up to me in a crowd
of people and asked, "Are you a Christian?" I was a little
surprised as to why he stopped me, but answered him that
I was in fact a follower of Jesus. He then looked at me with
great seriousness and said, "Please tell me what I have to do

to become a Christian!" He actually pulled out a large roll of money and tried to give it to me, if I would just tell him how to be a Christian.

I calmed the man down, and no, I did not take the money. I asked him what his story was. He told me that he was a Jewish man and had grown up his whole life in a Jewish neighborhood in Chicago. His parents had immigrated to the city and, because the Jewish population in Chicago is so large, they were able to move into a completely Jewish-concentrated neighborhood. His whole life he never interacted with anyone outside his Jewish community. He went to a Jewish school, Jewish synagogue, and shopped in Jewish markets. At one point after seeing something on TV about Christianity, he asked his parents about Jesus. His parents then threatened him, saying they would disown him if he was ever found with a Bible or seen talking to Christians. He grew up with both a fear and curiosity of Christianity, wondering what was so threatening about the life of Jesus that would cause his parents to be so fearful of a Christian's influence on him. This caused him to look at Christian material whenever he could find it, while keeping it a secret from his parents. However, he had never talked to a Christian himself.

I met him that day because he was visiting the county courthouse to finalize the inheritance of his parent's estate, after his last parent had just recently died. He walked out of the courthouse and realized for the first time that he was no longer restricted from talking to a Christian. He simply looked up and I was the first person he saw. I shared with him about Christ, why He had to come, and how Jesus was the Son of God. That day he accepted the Lord. We contacted a ministry that disciples Jewish believers and he was able to enter a new family. The whole encounter struck me as both exciting and unusual.

A few days later, we were in a completely concentrated South East Asian neighborhood on Chicago's North Side. In this community there were over 10,000 Vietnamese, Laotians, and Cambodians living in a six-square-block area. We had partnered with a small Vietnamese church to block off a street corner in their business district in order to perform dramas and share the gospel. After drawing a crowd with our dramas, the Vietnamese pastor interpreted our gospel message. We went out into the crowd to talk with people afterwards. Through one of our interpreters I talked with an elderly Vietnamese woman in her sixties. She told me she had lived in Chicago for forty years. She never learned English since she could function quite well in the neighborhood without it. She shopped at Vietnamese stores. All her neighbors were Vietnamese, and she worshiped at one of the Buddhist temples down the street from where she lived.

I asked her if she understood the drama and its message. I told her about the life of Jesus and what He came to do. She was very curious. She then asked me if this Jesus lived in Chicago and if she could meet him. Then it struck me. She had lived in Chicago for forty years and had never heard the name of Jesus. How could that be? I looked around the neighborhood and truly felt like I was in a different country. Here I was in the middle of a North American city, and all around me every sight, smell, and sound was completely foreign to my American culture.

Just north of the Vietnamese neighborhood we found other immigrant business districts that felt just as isolated. There was Little India, which catered to 300,000 Asian

Indians and Pakistanis living in the Chicago area. Next to that was Little Israel, servicing 250,000 Jews in Chicago. In our neighborhood were residential districts for Romanians, Somalis, Sudanese, Bosnians, Ethiopians, and Haitians, just to name a few. It was a regular occurrence to interact with dozens of different nationalities every time the team went out for ministry. One of the tools we used to dialogue with people in the community was a religious survey, which simply asked questions regarding what people believed about God. On average, a team of fifteen, who went to the nearest lakefront parks, would encounter thirteen different nationalities for every fifteen people they would stop. More surprisingly, of those thirteen different nationalities, eleven would be from the least evangelized nations of the world.

RECOGNIZING THE GIFT

As a missionary, I felt as if I had just received one of the greatest gifts that could have been given to the church. The nations that had been isolated from the gospel for centuries were now living within walking distance of where I was staying. It was this area that our permanent team moved into six months after our first outreach team arrived. In a five-mile radius around our YWAM housing, there are 350,000 people, of whom one out of three is foreign-born. There are as many as 150 nations living in this area. Down the street from us is a high school with fifty-three different languages spoken natively by the student body. One of five Chicagoans is now foreign born with over 100 different languages spoken in the public schools throughout the city.[2] In studies conducted by the U.S. Census, Chicago has averaged nearly 64,000 immigrants moving to the city every year,[3] creating 175 immigrants a day—7 an hour—moving into our neighborhoods. The most surprising reality is that almost half of those immigrants are from the least evangelized nations of the world.

As we discussed earlier, God has planted a "miracle" in every generation to give us access to the nations. Urbanization has created the greatest migration of isolated unreached peoples into reachable environments that the world has ever known. Surely this would not be the enemy's agenda. It is God who seeks to bring people out of isolation, while the devil seeks to keep them isolated. However, if the devil cannot keep them isolated, then he only needs to keep the church isolated from them. Is it possible that we are not aware of the greatest missions gift that has ever been given to the church? Are we not aware that the very people we are praying for are moving into our neighborhoods by the thousands on a daily basis?

There are now over 39 million foreign-born in the U.S. That makes one out of every eight people in America an immigrant.[4] This does not take into account the children of those immigrants, who though they may have been born in the U.S., are in fact living out a cultural lifestyle in their homes native to their parent's homeland. However, 92 percent of them live in our cities. Fifty percent live in our ten largest metropolitan areas, and one out of three of them live in our three largest cities: New York, Los Angeles, and Chicago.[5] According to a U.N. report on international migration, 175 million people are now living outside their country of birth, more than doubling from one generation ago.[6] One out of five of those are living in just twenty cities globally.[7] The largest gains were in North America with 1.4 million annually. It is urbanization that is drawing the unreached peoples of the world. Who is there to meet them? Urbanization could be seen as the greatest cross-cultural evangelism tool ever given to the church. Yet, as we saw in the story of the Vietnamese woman, these immigrants do not encounter the gospel by simply moving into a gospel-saturated culture. Instead they build cultural enclaves, allowing them the freedom to exist without interacting with people outside of their culture.

The only way we can partner with God in this opportunity is to actually move into the city and live among them. We need to redefine our mission. Make no mistake, we need to continue to train and send missionaries to the ends of the earth, seeking to establish a kingdom witness in every culture. However, we must mobilize a new generation of cross-culturally trained missionaries to the cities of the world or we risk passing up what could be our greatest tool in fulfilling the Great Commission. I will argue later that quite possibly the ones who will unlock the very isolated regions we seek to send missionaries to, already reside in our cities. However, the reports seem to indicate that we are slow to recognize the significance of this trend and may in fact be removing ourselves from its opportunity. In one five-year study performed by the U.S. Census, the metropolitan areas saw a migration of 6.8 million immigrants while losing a half million domestic residents. The top five metropolitan areas saw over 3.3 million new immigrants over five years, while 2.1 million domestic residents moved to nonmetropolitan areas.[8] The nations are coming to our back door by millions every year and we are moving away! Along with the 64,000 immigrants coming to Chicago every year, New York sees an average of 200,000; Los Angeles, 140,000; San Francisco, 75,000; and Washington DC, 60,000.[9]

Fourteen thousand immigrants a week are moving to

our ten largest cities in the U.S. while nearly nine thousand domestic Americans a week are leaving those same cities for more isolated environments.[10] As followers of Jesus and stewards of His vision to reach the nations, we cannot afford to leave the very places that the world is migrating to. The church was made to live near the nations. Has the enemy blinded us to this unprecedented gift? Are we trading our inheritance as God's people for safer and less costly environments?

This is not only a Western phenomenon. Global urbanization is also bringing the isolated people groups located within the developing nations of the world into their own cities, where they can be reached more effectively. Recently I was in a large international city in a religiously restricted nation. This city is growing by 200,000 people a year. Many of the people migrating to the city are from the hundreds of unreached people groups scattered throughout their own nation. I was meeting with a group of believers secretively in the city. This small underground church was made up of people from all over the countryside who had traveled to the city. I taught them about the parable of the lost son (Luke 15:11–32). I shared with them the significance of the gifts the father returned to the son when he came home, and how each of these gifts represented a returning of the son's identity and purpose. I then told them how this parable is a lesson for the nations. God has given every people group of the world a unique destiny to serve His purposes on the earth. He desires to give those callings and destinies back to the nations.

After our discussion, a woman in her forties began to weep. She shared with us that she was from a people group in the North. This particular people group is one of the unreached peoples of the world that still have yet to see a viable church witness in their culture. She and her husband had traveled many hundreds of miles to the city in order to study at the university. It was while she was at the university that she heard the gospel presented to her for the first time. She explained that no one in her village had ever heard the gospel. She became a believer through her new friendship with the Christian she had met. She then led her husband to the Lord, and they had been meeting with other believers and growing in their faith. For the past several months, however, they had begun to feel a burden for their village and the other villages in their home region that had never had the chance to hear the gospel.

While listening to the parable of the lost son, the Lord began to confirm to her heart that He had brought her to the city so that she could not only discover Him but also have the opportunity to take the gospel back to her people. That evening she declared that she and her husband were going to move back to this unreached region to share the gospel for the first time in that area. What happened next, I will never forget. The small group of twenty-five or so believers began to rally around this woman. They were all poor countryside believers, some of whom had been driven to the city because of their poverty. Yet they began to empty their pockets of money in order to raise an offering to send this couple back to their home so they could start a church-planting effort in one of the most unreached regions of the world. Even as I write this, my eyes are filled with tears. This was made possible because of urbanization. Our missionary God is moving the peoples of the world so that they may come in contact with the gospel. We simply need to recognize this generational gift and harness it, so that His purposes might be fulfilled.

AN ANSWER TO OUR PRAYERS

Remember that God is the missionary God. It is He who is most passionate about reaching the nations. He is most committed to seeing the Great Commission fulfilled and has the greatest knowledge of how to most effectively succeed in that task. Therefore, what is He doing that most effectively equips us to fulfill the calling He has given to His church? Every age is given a different paradigm and burden to advance the gospel in ways that the generation before did not. God's redemptive story on the earth is being built, brick upon brick, through the generations. In the late 1970s the church began to widely adopt a new paradigm that recognized the need to not only take the gospel to geo-political nations, but to the many distinct cultural and linguistic groups in those nations. In 1974 the Lausanne Congress on World Evangelism saw the church adopt this perspective in its overall mission. For the next several years mission agencies began to research and identify all the unreached people groups within nations, even developing materials allowing the church to pray for them individually. In 1985 the second Congress on World Evangelization took place, which emphasized further strategies for engaging these unreached people groups. At the same time that the Spirit of the Lord was giving this revelation to the church— to see isolated people groups of the world targeted with the gospel—we were experiencing the greatest migration of those peoples out of isolation into cities.

The People Profile Movement and Unreached People Groups initiatives of the 1980s and '90s began to mobilize large amounts of awareness and prayer for the remaining task of world evangelism. While the church was praying for ways to reach these isolated people groups, the three decades following the first Lausanne Congress saw 1.7 billion people migrate to cities, many from rural and isolated regions. While we prayed for these unreached peoples, they were sending their sons and daughters to the cities in order to survive. We went from 9.6 million foreign-born Americans in 1970 to 38.5 million in 2009.[11] In a little more than three decades almost 30 million immigrants moved to the U.S., with 92 percent in our cities. Prior to 1970, three out of four immigrants in the U.S. were of European decent. Yet in the last four decades they have represented only 10 percent of the 30 million who have arrived. One out of three of those who have arrived in the last thirty years have been from countries in Africa and Asia, representing some of the least evangelized nations of the world.[12] Once again, who was there to meet them? Why has our church growth for the last forty years in the U.S. been happening primarily outside the city? Why are most of our church planting strategies still primarily relevant only to rural or upper-middle class suburban environments? The ones we are praying for have been coming to us and we have not been there to meet them. Is it possible that though we vigorously adopted this new vision for world evangelism, with prayer initiatives and mission sending, we were not expecting God to do something on the earth that would be an answer to our prayers?

There are factors that cause people groups to remain isolated from the gospel. These factors can include things like a difficulty in geographic accessibility, political and governmental restrictions on outsiders, a lack of religious freedom, cultural isolation, ethnocentric phobias, and language barriers. Yet, each of these factors becomes substantially reduced when they migrate into the city. These isolated people groups are doing half the work for us; they remove the geographic isolation. Furthermore, because they need to survive relationally in the city they have migrated to, they are the ones pursuing friendship and contact with us. They need to understand the new culture into which they have entered in order to survive and become successful, and they seek to learn the language of the region they have migrated to. Out of several thousand ethnic surveys that we have done in the city, one of the largest needs expressed was a desire for friendships with the culture they had entered.

What we found was that these immigrants were most open to new friendships during the first six months to a year after arrival. It is during this time that they are most vulnerable and their needs most felt. They are eager to develop relationships, learn English, and understand the new culture they have found themselves a part of. They also have many felt needs that can become relational bridges to show them the love of Christ. Whoever they encounter during these first several months will become the greatest influence on them in either a positive or negative way. After the first year many have found connections with ethnic community enclaves that can keep them isolated. If they do not make new relationships quickly with the host environment they have entered, they will begin to entrench themselves in anything that can give them a sense of cultural survival. This will be a return to many of the things that kept them isolated to begin with. They will find a religious institution native to their homeland that they can cling to for cultural identity. They will likely move into ethnically concentrated neighborhoods and no longer feel the need to relate outside their culture for survival.

God has intended for the nations to come in contact with His people. The results of God's presence and blessing on His people always included the nations being drawn to them (Isa. 60:1–3). We must be the ones who meet them when they make the journey out of isolation. As the Lord continues to bring the unreached into the cities, we have an opportunity to partner with Him in being ready for their arrival. The U.N. predicts that the rural populations of all the nations of the world will continue to decrease and move to the cities every year for the next four decades.[13] We need a new generation of believers who can move into the urban mission field of the twenty-first century and recognize that God is bringing the harvest to them.

ANTICIPATING HIS PRESENCE

God loves the nations. We can have a confident expectation that His Spirit wants to reveal Himself when the nations are assembled. Before Jesus ascended to heaven, He told His followers to go into Jerusalem and wait for the arrival of His Spirit that the Father had promised. He did not, however, tell them when the Holy Spirit would come. In Acts 2 we see 120 of those followers waiting in an upper room in Jerusalem. As we discussed earlier, not only did the wisdom of God bring Jesus to the cross at an appointed time, but it is also that same wisdom that moves His church effectively until He returns.

When the Father decided to pour out His Spirit on the church, He chose the Day of Pentecost in Jerusalem. This was the one day in the Jewish calendar when all God-fearing Jews from every known nation would come to Jerusalem to celebrate. Can you see the wisdom of God in telling His followers to wait in the one geographical location where it was expected the nations would assemble? Is there any wonder why God chose the Day of Pentecost to reveal Himself to the church? He revealed Himself visibly to the nations that had gathered in Jerusalem. Furthermore, the Day of Pentecost was a harvest celebration. God not only chooses a place where a representation of the nations would be assembled, but also chooses the harvest celebration to make the connection between the outpouring of His Spirit and the harvest of the nations.

God's Spirit falls on His children and they begin to speak in all the languages of those who had gathered in the city. Why did God choose to do it this way? The outpouring of His Spirit was not just for His followers. It was to be a witness to the nations. They not only saw an outpouring of God's Spirit on people, but also discovered that He speaks their languages. Two things were declared in that moment that ushered in the new epoch of God's redeeming story. First, God's glory and presence would no longer dwell in temples but on men. We were to display His glory and carry His presence. Secondly, He was ready to display Himself as the God of all the nations, who would buy back their individual expressions. However, it must be noted that both of these revelations were intentionally applied in the context of unity. As the believers gathered in unity, God declared that it was in that context that His glory would rest. Likewise, as the nations assembled together, He would display a type of outpouring that would reveal Himself as a God of all the nations and redeemer of their unique individual expressions.

Just as God desires to reveal Himself and dwell in a

unified expression of His church, so does He desire to reveal Himself in a unified expression of the nations! This was the beginning of a new era in redemptive history. The first era could be seen as the filling of the earth and the development of the world's diversity. The second era was the selection of a nation to witness to other nations of how to discover a kingdom relationship with God in the context of their individuality. It was the development of the purpose of the nations and their relationship with their Maker. In this era, the Christ comes and brings a message of hope to all the nations. I would suggest that the third era, which Christ ushered in, is the time for the redemption of the nations and the bringing of the world's diversity into a context for a unified expression of God's image on the earth. It's the time for redeemed unity with diversity. Without this expression, the image of God could not be fully reclaimed in the human story.

How does He accomplish that witness on the earth? To be sure, God's agenda on the Earth will be both a context for the individual discovery of His image in the nations as well as a context for the discovery of His image in the relational unity between those individual nations. I submit that in that first outpouring of God's Spirit, He declared once and for all that His presence would be on people, His image would be revealed in the redemption of their cultures, and His habitation would be forever in the bringing together of that redeemed diversity. What we are witnessing in urbanization is a context, for the first time in human history, which can most adequately provide the habitation God's Spirit desires in the unity of the nations. For the first time since Pentecost, we are seeing a context on the earth, like we see in our cities today, where all the known nations of the world are assembling in geographical areas.

When I walk the streets of my city and see all the nations, I sense a desire of God's Spirit to reveal Himself to them. The nations are His. It is the redemption of those nations and the bringing them back into unity that He will forever marry Himself to. Whenever you see the nations assemble you can be confident that God wants to reveal Himself in that place. Yet, He only manifests himself through the unity of His followers (Matt. 18:20). In this new era of history, we are the temple of God. As Ephesians 2:22 says, "In him you too are being built together to become a dwelling in which God lives by his Spirit." Could it be that God is waiting for His people to come together, in the place the nations are assembling, so that He might pour Himself out in that place?

The nations of the world are coming to our cities. Whether to international gateway cities or regional cities within nations, the unreached, rural, and isolated people groups of the world are coming. This is a gift to the church. I am convinced that missionaries even one or two centuries ago would have given anything to have the access we have to the nations through our cities today. The opportunity of the city calls to the church. The city could be the very activity of our missionary God working with us, making us effective in the calling He has given us to reach the nations. This is our inheritance. We must not cast the cities aside.

Furthermore, if the nations are being brought together, who is preparing them to be a unified bride for the Lamb? As we will look at more deeply later, by urbanizing the planet, God is creating a context for the existence of a unified diverse expression of the nations. He is bringing His redemptive history to culmination. As His people gather in that place, it allows His presence to be manifested in that context. We have the opportunity to build a habitation for the Lord among all the diversity of the human story. God deserves the right to be manifested in that context. He alone gives meaning to its existence. He has wrapped this gift for us. It is time to unwrap it with Him.

Chapter 6
RELEASING A NEW MISSIONS GIFT

*The wealth on the seas will be brought to you, to
you the riches of the nations will come.*
—ISAIAH 60:5

*We cannot call a city to repentance without calling it
to ongoing purpose. The Gospel awakens the gift.*
—JOHN DAWSON[1]

WITHIN THE FIRST year of our arrival in Chicago,
I was invited to a Guatemalan Bible study group.
The families asked if I would come and speak to
them as they prepared to send out some of their group on
a mission trip. We all gathered in the living room of one
family's home. There were about ten young Guatemalans
there. They shared with me how the Lord had put the Arab
world on their heart. They not only had been praying for
Arab nations, but three of them had sensed the Lord's
direction to go as missionaries to the Middle East. They told
me how God had been speaking to them about the unique
gifting they had as Guatemalans to build relationships with
Arab peoples more easily than Americans. They asked me

to pray for these three missionaries, that they would go out with the strength and anointing of God. In that small living room we commissioned these young people to the Lord and the adventure they were about to enter with Him.

Something happened in my spirit that night. I had been a missionary for seven years and had worked in over a dozen different countries, yet I sensed an excitement for what the Lord was doing in a way I never had before. Here was a group of Guatemalans dreaming with God for the nations and discovering the unique gifting that He had given them in that mission. A new missions team was about to enter the unreached nations of the world; and rather than looking like white Euro-Americans, they were brown skinned and of Central American decent. What was making this possible? Guatemala is a poor country. How are they dreaming with God to go to the nations? The answer is urbanization.

The parents of these young people had immigrated to Chicago for work and a chance to build a different future for their children. Because of the opportunities they found in moving to the city, their children were now considering things that had never entered the minds of their parents. Cities create resources and access to tools that can enrich immigrants. Many come to our cities with a hope of obtaining the American Dream of individual success and affluence. But could there be another reason why the Lord has gifted the city with the acquisition and distribution of wealth? As the nations come to our cities, receiving education, training, and wealth, can they be encouraged to dream a different purpose for these forms of blessing than the self-centeredness of an American Dream? Who will be there to help them dream that dream?

RECLAIMING THE VALUE OF THE NATIONS

All the nations have a unique priestly and kingdom duty (Rev. 5:10). If God were to restore the honor and glory of the nations on the earth, how would He do that? The redemptive purposes of God in the nations include not only the restoration of His relationship to those nations, but also the restoration of their ability to love and honor Him with their unique designs. Unless we anticipate the restoration of all the nations' unique gifts, as a part of God's redeeming work on the earth, we will not look for the ways in which His Spirit is orchestrating that end. If our present era of history is the time for the reclaiming and restoring of God's purpose for the nations, there must be something that God is providing that will ensure its possibility.

Not only has urbanization brought the nations out of isolation into reachable environments, but it has also created a context by which those people groups can now bless other nations. Definition and vision must be given to this possibility if we are to fulfill God's redeeming purposes on the earth. The modern city creates a setting for the interrelating of the nations. In my neighborhood of Rogers Park in Chicago, there are eighty different language groups. In the two-mile radius around our YWAM building there are over one hundred different nationalities. Not only are the nations coming out of isolation, but they are also moving in proximity to the rest of the nations. Pakistanis are living next to Indians, Jewish immigrants next to Arabs, and Bosnians next to Serbians and Croatians. These nations have all had a history of great conflict with each other. Urbanizing them into more neutral urban areas has created the opportunity to display reconciliation and healing among these nations.

The church alone has the vision and capacity to help facilitate that goal.

Furthermore, as people groups seek refuge and new beginnings in the city, an opportunity is created to teach and facilitate their unique gifts back around the world, through the resources gained in that city. Surely God desires to bless the people groups of the world, but that blessing is made complete by giving back to them their unique honor of blessing other nations. Is it possible that God is urbanizing the planet in order to reclaim this honor for the nations? In recent years, missiologists have begun to discover that different cultures have access into some cultures more than others. Pacific Asian Islanders have seen great responses from Native Americans. Native Americans have seen unusual success among Jews as well as Mongolians. As I mentioned before, some Latin American cultures are seeing great success among Arab cultures. African-Americans have received an amazing welcome among some of the Baltic States, and Asian Indians have seen an unusual bridge into many African people groups.

These are just a few examples of how nations are gifted uniquely to minister to other nations. How many other examples are waiting to be discovered? Because of urbanization, nations and people groups are being forced to live next to each other in ways that they would have never done otherwise. This experience can become a discovery of the very riches and wealth of the nations, which are the people themselves. The reclaiming and facilitating of the unique honor of the nations often presents two major roadblocks: its discovery and the acquisition of resources needed to facilitate it. It is the very nature of the city to meet both of these needs. By bringing the nations together in relational proximity, we are able to discover the cultural bridges that exist among them. As these nations gain education, training, and resources in the city, they are able to dream with the Lord about the unique callings and destinies He has for them. We as the church have the opportunity to help nurture and facilitate this process.

STEWARDING THE GIFT

The city functions like a heart. It pulls in and thrusts out the lifeblood of a nation. It is the gift of a city to facilitate both the coming in of the wealth of the nations and its going out. All that is needed is a heavenly kingdom vision for this process, and for God's people to steward its potential. One of our most significant ethnic communities in Chicago is our South Asian district. There are more Asian Indians in Chicago than in any city outside of India. One of our first ethnic neighborhood outreaches was focused on this community. Along with evangelism strategies in the neighborhood, we developed relationships with a number of Indian believers. We started a weekly Bible study with Indian youths between the ages of fifteen and thirty. Almost all of these were second-generation Indians. Their parents had immigrated to Chicago in hopes of securing a better future for their children. Because of the hard work of their parents, these Indian young people were now studying to become everything from doctors to software technicians.

If you looked at these Indians, you would think they were just like all other middle-class American kids. However, in their homes, they were living a cultural identity native to India. Many were struggling to understand both their Indian identity and American identity. We met weekly for several years. We talked about the character of God, His purpose for man, and the glory He wanted to redeem in the nations. You could see that they began to hunger for their identity in the Lord. After a couple of years we took a number of them on a missions trip to El Salvador. This was our first time bringing an all-ethnic team from Chicago to the mission field. It was always humorous to see the reactions of the El Salvadorians when our team would walk through their village. They didn't know where to place them; they didn't look American, but they didn't look Latino either. Every home was opened to this team of Asian Indians. They had the attention of everyone they talked to. I had never experienced this kind of a response on any of the all-white Euro-American mission teams I had been on before.

Once again I experienced a monumental turning point in my understanding of missions. I realized that these Asian Indians were able to minister in ways that I could not. I had traveled to India before and visited many believers there. Yet, when I talked to them about their role in going to the nations, I did not see the same hope and excitement that I saw in these young Indians from Chicago. What was the difference? By the time our team returned from Central America, they were already discussing where the Lord might want them to go next. What gave these young Indians an ability to dream about their role in missions differently than their counterparts in India? The urbanization of their parents, and the resources they had obtained through that migration to a city had created the ability for these young people to dream in ways their forefathers had not.

Before we had begun to instill that God-given dream in them, however, they had not even considered the possibility. When we shared the vision with Indian churches in Chicago to raise money for sending this team out, it was often met with looks of disbelief. The sentiment was, "Why should we spend money to send these Indian youths to other nations, when our nation is so needy?" Most of the Indian churches felt that missions was still primarily a Euro-American privilege and responsibility. It didn't stop these Indian youths, though. The next year we took them to Haiti. The Haitians absolutely loved these Indians. They also could not place them at first; most thought that perhaps they were wealthy French Haitians. Yet because of their curiosity, every home was opened to them. Again, I had been to Haiti on mission trips before but had never experienced this kind of welcome.

The most exciting times in Haiti were when our team was able to speak in churches. The Indian youths would stand in front of these churches and tell them that they were from the poorest country in the Eastern Hemisphere, and God had sent them to the nations with the honor of bringing the gospel. They would then encourage these Haitian believers that though they were from the poorest nation in the Western Hemisphere, God could give them back their honor among the nations as well. The churches would come unglued at this. They would jump from their seats and begin to shout and scream praise to God. I could not have gotten that same response as a white American. God is ready to redeem the honor of the nations in our day. Urbanization is creating that opportunity.

Our next outreach was to a small town in Oklahoma with a high concentration of Native Americans, where we saw the same kind of response. What took place next, however, was probably the most life changing for the group. The next year we took nearly twenty Indians from Chicago on outreach to India. These young people began to feel a great significance for their identity as Indians before the Lord. Many had been to India before but just to visit family. This time they were traveling to India to minister God's love to the Indian people and bring them the hope that they had discovered. Every morning we met to pray for the people of India, and I could see a deep burden developing on our team. As they ministered to the believers, you could see our team carrying a deep desire to see the honor of the Indian people restored in the Lord. They shared in churches and encouraged the believers to dream with God and have faith that God could use them to reach the nations, simultaneously realizing the struggle that these believers faced economically in considering that dream.

At the end of our outreach, we began praying about the unique gifting on India to the nations and where God may want to send them next. They felt that they were to believe God to go to Uganda. Yet, something was different this time. They not only wanted to believe God for the finances to go themselves, but to raise money for the chance to have several believers from India meet us on the mission field as well. Our team from Chicago would trust God for the airfares to see several come from India while encouraging them to raise the two hundred dollars per person for their ground fees in Africa. The next year we had twelve Indians from Chicago and eight Indians from India converge together in Uganda. This was the most fulfilling mission outreach I had ever been on. Not only did we see incredible opportunities for ministry from these Indians to the Ugandans, but there was also a sense of holy awe over what was taking place.

This is a picture of the modern missions movement. It's the time for the redeeming of the nations' place and honor in the Great Commission. The nations of the world will not be reached with the gospel until we see the unique gifts of all the nations enter the mission field. Some of these Indian youths have been a part of full-time mission work now, and others are dreaming with God about how their professions can be used to bless the nations. I would submit that it is the phenomenon of urbanization that has made this story and others like it around the globe possible. No longer can we simply go to the mission field alone as white Euro-Americans. We must seek to take the wealth of the nations with us, or we will not be able to finish the Great Commission.

More than 690,000 immigrants came to the U.S. last year just to study in the universities, most of which are located in our cities, with one out of three students coming from China and India alone.[2] Can we be there to help them gain a greater vision for their education than just the furtherance of their individual lifestyles? With over a million immigrants moving to U.S. cities each year, is there anyone there who can meet them and give them a dream bigger than the American Dream? Is it possible that by stewarding this wealth of the nations well, we could see the release of the greatest, most effective missionary force the world has ever seen?

THE KEY TO FINISHING THE TASK

In the previous chapter I shared the story of the Asian woman who, after encountering the gospel in a city, felt the burden to take it back to those who had never heard in her homeland. Often it is those who have come out of the unreached regions of the world who, after experiencing the Lord, feel the greatest burden to go back with the love of

Christ. Let me tell you about Mohamed. Recently, one of the young Indians who had been on several of our mission trips was sitting in a McDonalds restaurant a few blocks from our YWAM building. He noticed a young Senegalese man sitting with his luggage in a booth nearby. The young African looked frightened and alone. Normally, our Indian friend would not have approached someone like this. However, because the Lord had given him a heart for the nations after traveling with us around the world, he felt compelled to get involved. He discovered that Mohamed had recently come to the U.S. on a refugee visa, and had traveled from his host city to Chicago to try to find a relative who could help him. After arriving in Chicago, he discovered that his family was no longer there, and he had been sleeping on the streets for two nights, not knowing what to do.

Our friend told him about us and that we had housing that was often used to take in immigrants who were in need. He then called me. We had another Senegalese man living with us who had been a Muslim and became a believer. Together we went to the McDonalds and invited Mohamed to come and stay with us until he could work things out. The young boy was frightened, but came with us. He did not say a word to me the whole way to the apartment. After I showed him his bed, introduced him to the other immigrants in the building, and told him that we would begin the next day trying to find out what assistance we could get for him, he finally spoke. He asked why we were doing this. I told him that we were followers of Jesus and that we believed God loved all the nations and wanted us to take care of those in our city. He looked at me with a puzzled look and asked if we knew that he was a Muslim. I told him I assumed that he was since his name was Mohamed. He said, "But you are Christians." He just kept shaking his head and saying that he doesn't know why we would take him in. He contacted some of the Muslims of the Senegalese community in Chicago and they would not do anything for him. He couldn't understand why we, being Christians, would care for him in this way.

Over the weeks that followed, he asked many questions about Jesus. He watched the Jesus film[3] several times and read completely through a French New Testament we had given him. Every day, he would ask us questions. At one point Jesus visited him in a dream and he dramatically accepted the Lord. He began to get discipled and grow in the Lord. He was so hungry to know Jesus and follow him wholeheartedly. Almost daily he would make changes in his actions after discovering on his own that they would not be pleasing to God. Then the moment came. I began to see him struggling. He would talk to his family on the phone in Senegal, and then show a distressed attitude. He approached me one day and told me that he needed to go back to Senegal. He felt a burden for his family. As far as he knew, no one in his village had heard the gospel. His mom had just passed away, and he could not bear thinking of anyone else in his family not experiencing what he had found in Jesus. He was in the U.S. on a refugee visa; if he went home, he would never be able to get that visa again. The average annual income for families in Senegal is about three hundred U.S. dollars. Many in his family were hoping that he would make money in the U.S. and be able to support the village. Yet, he felt overwhelmingly compelled of the Lord to give that all up in order to take the gospel back to this unreached region of the world.

We actually tried to discourage him at first. After all he was a new believer and we weren't sure he understood what it would cost him. He was determined, though, and the burden to take the gospel back to his people was one that he was willing to trade his own comfort and safety to satisfy. We took him to the airport and prayed over him. I wasn't sure what was going to happen. A couple of months later, I received a message from him, which said that he had found a church that was a two-hour walk from his village. He was getting involved in that church and sharing the gospel with his family. He assured me that he was going to stay faithful to the Lord.

The story of Mohamed is an urban story. The factors involved in this story were made possible because of urbanization. Mohamed found himself in a city because of his refugee status. A second-generation immigrant who had discovered his destiny to the nations through his involvement in missions, felt compelled to get involved in the life of this young African now living near him in the city. We were able to bridge a gap to Mohamed because of another Senegalese man who had come out of Islam and now has a burden to reach other Muslims in the city. After Mohamed discovered Christ he became burdened to take the gospel back to his homeland.

This is the gift of the city in operation. When the nations come out of isolation to a city, they are given an opportunity to discover the Lord and His calling on their lives. Furthermore, the redemption of their unique gifting in the Lord finds a context by which they can bless the nations around them strategically, and extend the gospel back around the world in ways it could not have been otherwise. How many more urban stories like this could be taking place in the nations if we simply harnessed the gift that is the city? The city provides access to the nations, a context by which the gifts of the nations can bless each other, and the resources to mobilize those nations strategically back around the world. This is a gift to missions, not a hindrance.

There are still nearly two billion people who are isolated from the gospel. These nations are hard to reach because of geography, culture, governmental restrictions, and language. What is God doing to help eliminate these barriers and equip His people with the tools needed to reach them? God is giving His church access through new miracles of communication and technology. Yet, one of the most effective keys to unlocking the unreached peoples of the world are those who were previously unreached people, who have come out of the darkness, and can now bring the authority of Jesus back. As these immigrants to the city discover Jesus, they are equipped with the culture, language, and access needed to bridge the gaps into their homelands as well as other unreached regions. Psalms 127:1 reminds us, "Unless the LORD builds the house, its builders labor in vain." We must determine the blueprints for success that the Lord had designed if we are to finish the task of world missions. We must apply the tools that the Lord has given us to release His purposes in the nations. We know now that the job will not get done with just Euro-American believers; we simply do not have the access or gifting to reach all the unreached peoples of the world. We need to put the right keys in the locks. Those keys are being brought to our cities by the millions every week. It's time to steward that gift.

A WILLINGNESS TO PAY THE PRICE

Karim came to stay in our immigrant housing a couple of years ago. He is from a very restricted Middle Eastern Nation.

He had acquired an asylum visa, and after going through hardship, he now had a visa that would allow him to stay and work in the U.S. for the rest of his life. He accepted the Lord while staying in our Christian community. It was such a joy to watch his love for the Lord. He showed so much joy and passionate desire in his new life in Jesus. He always had a smile on his face. However, he quickly began to be tested in his new faith. When his family back home discovered that he had become a Christian, they threatened him with the loss of his inheritance and family. He told me one day that he felt it was a test to see how much he really loved Jesus. He was determined to stay loyal to the Lord. And then it happened. He too began to carry a deep burden for his family and village back home. He would talk to them on the phone and try to convince them of the new life he had in Jesus. But it wasn't enough. "If only I could go back, I could show them Jesus," he would say to me. He declared one day that the Lord had put it on his heart to return home. I told him that if he did this he could never come back to this country under his asylum status. He would be giving up a future and security. He simply said that it was a small price to pay to bring the gospel to his family.

He searched and found a church somewhere near his village and contacted that pastor by phone. He told him his story and asked the pastor to find out what the legal ramifications would be in his country if he came back after leaving on asylum. The pastor looked into this, and told him that the average sentence seemed to be two years in prison once he returned. Karim came to me excitedly and said that he could do that. He was willing to go to prison if he could just take the gospel back to his homeland. The prisons in this country are some of the worst in the world, especially for political dissenters. Yet Karim found it bearable if he could just share Jesus with his family.

Like Mohamed, we prayed over Karim and sent him out not knowing what would happen to him. He left with a smile on his face, giving up all the security and possible future of an American Dream. I did not hear from him for almost two months. I got a call from him on Christmas Day. He was so excited. He kept saying, "Praise the Lord, praise the Lord." He told me that he had not been arrested at the airport. He met the pastor of this small church and had been openly sharing the gospel around his town. Once again the gift of urbanization was bearing fruit in the nations.

The significance of Karim's story is in the way that he responded to the gospel, and his willingness to embrace sacrifices in order to take that gospel back to his home. Not only do white Euro-Americans lack all the cultural bridges needed to reach many of the isolated peoples of the world, but often find the sacrifices needed to reach those areas unbearable. Karim had access to that unreached region in ways I did not. Even greater, he was able to embrace the hardships more readily than I would in order to take the gospel to his people. The key is the level of burden felt. Karim had a natural capacity to carry a burden for his people in ways I could not have. These are the key players in finishing the task of the Great Commission. God has designed us to carry burdens for our families and nations. He is bringing these people to us.

Living and walking among us in our cities are the keys to the nations. They want to develop relationships with us. They are making the journey of bridging their cultures to ours. They are doing much of the work for us in the challenges of reaching the unreached. It is our glory as the church to live among them and steward this gift. God is laboring with us to finish the task of world evangelism. Yet I fear that much of the treasure still remains hidden from God's people. The enemy works hard to keep us blinded to the reality and magnitude of the miracle that God has provided for His followers. If 92 percent of the immigrants coming to our nation are living in our cities, then it's to the cities we must go. By doing so, we may find the very tools God has designed to reach the remaining unreached peoples of the world.

Chapter 7
A PLACE FOR HEALING

There is a river whose streams make glad the city of God, the holy habitation of the Most High.
—PSALMS 46:4, ESV

In modern cities shalom is attacked and undermined in a thousand ways, and therein lies the root of urban problems.
—ROGER GREENWAY[1]

B ROKENNESS LIKES A certain level of isolation. It's precisely the shame and insecurity of our brokenness that cause us to seek controlled environments. Perhaps this is what it means for man to love darkness rather than the light (John 3:19). We use darkness to hide our fear, shame, and insecurity. What Adam and Eve did in the Garden, when they hid from God, has been the tendency of mankind ever since. We seek those environments that threaten us the least and we can control the most. By doing so, we can build the illusion that everything is OK and not face the shame of our brokenness. However, God was not satisfied to leave Adam and Eve in their hiding, and He works throughout the ages to continue to bring us into the light. God is a redeemer by nature. He says in Isaiah 63:16, "Our Redeemer from of old is your name." This means that He has a jealous desire and commitment to buy back what has been stolen in our lives and restore to us the wholeness He originally intended. It is this commitment that moves God to bring our brokenness into the light so that He can heal us.

In Acts 17:27, Paul reminds us that God is determining the places that we live, in hopes that we may grope for Him and find Him, though He is not far from any one of us. Have you ever felt like God put you in a situation that forced your fears and insecurities to the surface? Has it not been those moments when we were forced to face the shame of our brokenness that we most found healing? God is not afraid to put us in situations that will bring to the light the very things He desires to heal and restore. What have you found that most effectively exposes your hidden fears and brokenness? Is it not relational pressure, and proximity to what threatens us in other people, that most shouts to us? When we attempt community without wholeness and the grace of the Lord, it is a failed experiment every time. Ironically, however, it is intense community and proximity to relational pressures that most reveals the areas we are still broken in. This is the gift of the city.

By urbanizing the planet, God is creating the most intense context for relational pressure in order to bring to the light what He is ready to heal in the nations. When we think of cities, we often think of people who are impersonal or rude. It seems that no one wants to talk to anyone else. Thousands of people pass by each other every day without making eye contact. Yet after living in the city for nearly twenty years, I have discovered that this is actually a defense mechanism.

People are overwhelmed by their inability to relate, their insecurity and inability to control those relationships, and the lack of internal resources to keep up with all the relational stimulus being thrown at them. In other words, it's the moment-by-moment opportunities to interact with so much relational dynamic and diversity that shout to us how broken and unprepared we are. The city is not only a definition of what we were created for, but also the very witness of how far we have fallen from that design. In order to survive we simply build filters to keep out all the pressure to relate and the threatening intrusion of others wanting to relate when we feel so empty inside.

It is the mercy of God to put us in these hothouse environments to keep us from making artificial coverings for ourselves and force us to face our shame and brokenness. His goal is that we might search and grope for Him. Not only is God urbanizing the planet to define for us what we are being prepared eternally for, but also to reveal to us how unprepared for that home we are. It is this revelation that is meant to cause us to cry out for Him so He might heal us. The city can be a place of healing. It's a place to discover both our brokenness and the One who can make us whole. However, since God's children are the agents of His presence and healing, unless we exist in these hothouse environments we will not come in contact with the brokenness of the nations.

When we think of cities, we also think of all the sinful perversion and deceptions leading people astray. These are simply the desperate attempts to fill the voids and insecurities that shout so loudly at the urban dweller. Again, it is the cry of the Lord in Ezekiel 22:29–31, reminding us that He is looking for His people to stand in the gap and build up walls of protection around the injustices of broken community.

In his book *Taking our Cities for God*, John Dawson talks about the disorientation that the average urban dweller faces. He adds that "because of the disorientation they experience, urban dwellers are extremely vulnerable to both sweeping revival and mass deception through some false hope. The city dweller is often an idolater. The city intensifies everything, and this includes devotion to false gods."[2] Most people living in cities are very religious. Their religion can be a wide variety of thought. They adopt philosophies and religious activities to help them survive an environment whereby their fears and insecurities can no longer be hidden. The pressures of city life and intense community push you to become spiritual. Yet unless the church is there to direct them toward a true hope, they are forced into an endless cycle of false hopes and failed security.

LIVING NEXT TO THE BROKENNESS

The average urban dweller is like a boiling pot waiting to boil over on the first willing listener they come in contact with. This is the environment that God's people were designed to live in. We are the agents of God's hope and restoration. However, you cannot predict when the pot will boil over. The blessing of living in close proximity to the brokenness of the world is that you are there when it is brought into the light. Because our team lived in apartment buildings, we saw what people were going through on a daily basis. I have already mentioned how we would have to call the police at times to keep the domestic violence in check that was going on down our hall. One couple a few doors down from ours seemed to be in fights all the time. The man believed his wife was prostituting herself when he wasn't around. Whenever we would hear it getting out of hand, I would go down the hall and let them know that, though we understood they were working things out, we would call the police if at anytime it sounded like he was hitting her.

One day, he came home and started in on her again. I looked out my door and saw their two kids, who were about four and six years old, standing in the hall with their heads down. They stood there, frightened, as their parents yelled at each other. I went down the hall and asked them if their kids could come down to our apartment and play with our kids until they worked things out. They kind of nodded *whatever,* and we took the kids to our apartment. We brought out toys and they played on the floor. They were a little timid at first but then began to relax and have fun. It was a chance for them to find some peace in the turmoil that was so common in their lives. This is what it looks like to "build up the broken down walls." As the mother came to get the kids later, it became an opportunity to encourage her and let her know that we are always there.

Below our apartment was a single mom who had a live-in boyfriend. We discovered later that she was actually a prostitute and her live-in boyfriend was the one arranging her business. She had a four-year-old boy from one of her encounters, and didn't even know who the father was. Because our team members went out of the way to talk to her and be kind to her, she ended up knocking on our door one day. She was in tears and said she didn't know where to go for help. Her boyfriend had been threatening her to go out and work. She had to go to a "job interview" that day and didn't know what to do with her son. Though we lived in a fifty-unit apartment building, she came upstairs to our apartment because she said we were the only ones she felt she could trust. Of course we let the boy stay with us, and this became an ongoing opportunity to pray and minister to this woman.

The church is designed to live next to the brokenness of the world, not isolated from it. If we remove the presence of God's people from those environments that expose men's broken lives, then who will be the salt and light to those in need? We as God's people have strategized and labored to find that perfect evangelism model that can reach into people and stir up hunger for God. Yet, the most effective model in Scripture has been presence. As we live in proximity to the world, God is able to bring out the world's desperation in front of His people. We then are able to partner with how God's Spirit has already stirred the hearts of people, and we simply become those who lead them to Jesus. The pressure of urban life in the modern city can be an asset to the church. Involvement in people's lives and the possibilities of evangelism are thrust at you in the city on a daily basis.

Often, just leaving the apartment to go to the corner store would bring you in contact with some issue of brokenness in someone's life. It was a running joke for my wife and I that whenever I said I was going to the corner for something and would be right back, she would laugh and say, "We'll see." One time I went out our building's front door with a couple friends to get milk, and a woman with blood all over her hands just fell on me. She was hysterical and it took us awhile to calm her down. It turned out she had gone down the street to get a cheap abortion in an alley and was hemorrhaging. All of a sudden we were thrust into her situation, whether we wanted to or not.

Another time I opened my door to find two grown men fighting in our hallway. I knew these men; they were from an apartment down the hall and I thought they were friends. I had to jump in the middle of them, because one man had the other on the floor and was drawing blood by kicking him in the head with his boot. They were both immigrants from Romania. It turns out that they were having dinner together and one of them made a racial slur against Gypsies. The other man was of Gypsy descent and became enraged. All this pent-up rage from generations of racism came out. That encounter turned into an opportunity to talk with these men over the next several days about reconciliation and forgiveness.

It would simply take too long to tell you of all the encounters over the years. I am convinced that the enemy has worked so hard to keep God's children intimidated by the city so that the very agents of God's healing for the nations could not come in contact with the world. The neighborhoods that we are often afraid to live in are the very environments that God wants to use to push people towards Him. We need a generation willing to live among and relate to all the relational dynamics created by the city, truly being a light in the darkness.

CONNECTING THE CITY TO GOD

I have found that because the city naturally makes people aware of their fears and insecurities, one of the most effective ways to minister to the city is through prayer evangelism. Over the years we have found creative ways to pray for people on the streets, whether in parks, on buses, on street corners, or in plazas. A number of years ago the Lord led us to send teams to one of the busiest plazas in our downtown business district. Daley Plaza is the site of Chicago's largest courthouse building and is also located next to the city's government buildings and office complexes. During the lunch hours every day, thousands of people walk through the plaza. We would simply walk around the plaza and ask people if they needed prayer for anything. We had gotten the idea of setting up "Prayer Stations" in our city from the YWAM Metro New York Team.[3] Quite honestly, when we began doing this over fourteen years ago, I had real doubts as to whether anyone would actually stop and talk to us. However, from the very first team we sent there until now, I have been consistently amazed at the response.

Our teams have prayed for more than 20,000 people in that plaza. A team of about fifteen will pray with over one hundred people in less than two hours. I am also amazed by the level of desperate need total strangers are willing to divulge to our team members. There always seem to be people that God has prepared especially for our arrival, as if He is just waiting for His children to go and direct these people to His heart for them. Businessmen have opened up about failed marriages and children they are losing to the temptations of the world. Judges and lawyers have asked for wisdom in difficult cases they are involved in. People have opened up about abuses in relationships, a need of healing for a loved one, or some desperate financial crisis.

In each of these situations, we have the opportunity to pray with them right there on the street. When a person opens his heart up to the Lord, if even in a small way, something supernatural happens. The presence of God's Spirit is allowed to invade their thoughts and emotions. Often businessmen and women, affluent or working class, are in tears by the time we finish praying. The city is not only desperate for help but also desperate for the presence of God. Prayer is the supernatural act of connecting people to God's Spirit. Ironically, some of the ones who open up the most are those who seem distant and want to be alone. The vulnerability that causes people to withdraw also reminds them of their need constantly. We simply bring God's people in proximity to that need. That is the gift of the city.

I try to go with these teams every time they go to Daley Plaza. I have seen such a readiness in the Lord to reveal Himself to people. Again, it's as if He is the One who has orchestrated their inability to hide any longer, and is waiting for the opportunity to introduce Himself to them. After arriving in the plaza one day, I sent the teams out and looked up to ask someone if I could pray for them. I noticed a well-dressed woman coming out of the courthouse about twenty yards away. I felt led to go and talk to her. As I walked toward her, she stopped and stared at me with a disconcerting look. The closer I got, the more she looked at me with disbelief. I walked up to her and asked if there was anything we could pray for her that day. She had a look of shock on her face and asked, "What did you say?" I told her that there was a group of us who had come to the plaza to pray for people, and that the Lord had sent us to give people hope. I didn't normally say that, it just came out. She took a gasp, got teary eyed, and said, "I don't know if you believe in this or not, but I think I had a vision of you last night!"

The woman told me how she had gone through a difficult divorce, lost her job, and had recently been evicted from her apartment. Because of this, she was in court fighting to keep custody of her children. The night before we met, she had been so depressed by the loss in her life that she was going to commit suicide. Just before taking an overdose of pills, she felt an overwhelming presence in the room and a sense that God was sad about what she was going to do. This had actually made her angry. She yelled at God and told Him that she was not even sure if He existed, but that she had no reason to live. She said she had this mental picture of her walking out of the courthouse and meeting someone who looked like me. That person told her that God had sent him to give her hope. Again frustrated, she told God that unless that happened the next day when she was at the courthouse, she was going to kill herself.

You can imagine the openness that I had with this woman, sharing with her about God's heart for her and the hope of restoration that He could bring in her life. We talked about Jesus and His commitment to her. She prayed with me and cried out to the Lord. She told me afterwards, with tears coming down her face, that I could not understand how much our meeting had changed her life. Once again I was amazed at the way God orchestrates these encounters. Recently I stopped a very affluent looking businessman walking from work and asked if I could pray for Him about anything. He actually looked at me with a stunned look and stuttered some response. I asked again, but his eyes just got watery and he could not speak. After a few moments, he finally told me in a struggled whisper that he was going through a difficult divorce and he just wanted his wife back. We prayed together as this grown man wept in the middle of downtown Chicago.

We have done such a good job isolating ourselves from the world. People are desperate. The glory of the church is to live among them. There are so many stories of how God has met people on buses and park benches, in coffee shops and Laundromats. So often we curse the city because of all of its crowdedness and relational intrusions. Yet, this is the very environment that God uses to reveal our need of Him. It is a tool that God's children can use to find access into people's broken lives.

THE FIELD THAT IS RIPE FOR HARVEST

In Matthew 9:35–38 we read a familiar passage. It begins with a description of Jesus' activities. He has just finished going through towns and villages, "Teaching in their synagogues, preaching the good news of the kingdom and healing every disease and sickness" (v. 35). It then says that when He saw the crowds He had compassion on them, because "they were harassed and helpless, like sheep without a shepherd" (v. 36). There is a reaction evoked in the heart of Jesus when He sees these crowds of people. He feels compassion for them. The Greek word actually means to make your bowls yearn with longing.[4] The redeeming heart of God is stirred by the brokenness of people. What bothers the Lord is that these people are weak from being driven and tossed about like sheep without a shepherd. In other words they are being harassed by life without anyone to direct them to the good path and gentle stream. This is the role that God desires to have in our lives.

It is with this revelation concerning the crowds that Jesus turns to His followers and declares that "the harvest is plentiful but the workers are few"(v. 37). I would suggest that this statement is made not as a general remark concerning mankind but in direct response to the state of the people He was witnessing. The Lord was in fact defining for His followers the kind of field that is ripe and ready for harvesting. Whenever you see throngs of people who are being driven and harassed by life with a lack of direction and hope, you are witnessing a field that God has made ready to be reaped. We simply need to "ask the Lord of the harvest, therefore, to send out workers into his harvest field" (v. 38).

The definition that the Lord gives us for a field that is ripe for harvest is the definition of the city. The city drives people and harasses them. Because of so many things vying for their attention, people are overloaded with options. The city can be an endless pursuit of good pasture and healing streams, without anyone to help them navigate through the endless options that are bombarding them. The average urban dweller is reminded daily of failed promises and the inability to secure a future and a hope. This is the environment that cries out for leadership. The streets and dwellings of the modern city are crying out for someone who can bring direction and hope. This is our harvest field. It is the field that God has made ready! It is time for the workers to be sent!

Chapter 8
RIDING THE NEW WAVE OF MISSIONS

*And this gospel of the kingdom will be
preached in the whole world as a testimony to
all nations, and then the end will come.*
—MATTHEW 24:14

*Cities are the places where the destinies of nations
are determined. Cities are the centers of communication, commerce, cultural life, and government. As the
cities go, so go the nations. If winning the nations to
Christ is our assignment, to the cities we must go.*
—ROGER GREENWAY[1]

TWO THOUSAND YEARS ago Jesus commissioned His
followers to co-labor with Him in the plan to restore
His original intent for mankind. He declared, "Go
and make disciples of all nations, baptizing them in the
name of the Father and of the Son and of the Holy Spirit,
and teaching them to obey everything I have commanded
you" (Matt. 28:19–20). Jesus defined His mission for His
followers. It was a clear call of what His agenda was to be
through His church. Three distinct mandates are given.

First, we were to be about making disciples of the nations. The word for nations here is *ethnos*.[2] It is where we get the word for ethnic groups. There was not only an individual application to this command but a corporate application as well. As we looked at before, there are corporate identities that God wishes to redeem. He has created the diversity of the nations and intends that their unique expressions would be brought back into their original purpose and design. The word *disciple* means to teach or instruct. The followers of Jesus are to be about instructing the nations in righteousness and the dreams that God had for them when they were brought into existence. Second, we are given the mandate to baptize (immerse or submerge[3]) these nations in the person and life of the Father, Son, and Holy Spirit. Finally, we are told to teach these nations to obey all that the Lord had commanded the disciples while He was with them.

This last command of Jesus before ascending into heaven released a new era of human history. It was to be the redeeming of the nations and the bringing into restoration all that God had originally intended for the human story. The question is, how do we fully complete this Great Commission? The history of God's people for the last two millennia has been a story of how well we were either reaching that goal or being slowed down in its fulfillment. Perhaps the most fascinating period of that mission history has been the last few hundred years.

Though the gospel spread decisively throughout the different parts of the known world, from the time of Christ until the modern age, the modern mission movement of the last 250 years has by far been the most successful. In an article of the book *Perspectives on the World Christian Movement*, Ralph Winter characterizes the three distinct waves of modern mission focus and mobilization.[4] A man named William Carey pioneered the first wave. The revelation he brought to the church in the late eighteenth century was an understanding that the gospel must be taken to the unreached "coastlands" of the continents of the world if we were to fulfill the Great Commission. Though this was met with much opposition, the growing awareness of the needs of these unknown lands and a movement of passionate young people towards these coastlands brought phenomenal growth to the church. It was an era of great sacrifice. Most missionaries died within the first or second year.

During the later half of the nineteenth century, a man named Hudson Taylor brought the second wave of modern missions to the forefront. As believers were celebrating the success on the coasts of new lands, Taylor was challenging the church with the need to take the gospel farther "inland." This was the period of Inland Missions. This revelation that the gospel would never reach the isolated regions of the interiors unless people went, once again ignited the passions and commitments of another generation of young people. It took twenty to forty years for this new paradigm to take root. Over forty agencies started, many as faith-based and nondenominational because of the many organized churches that disagreed with the wisdom of going into these interiors. A new and larger student mobilization was launched with the "Student Volunteer Movement for Foreign Missions." Over 100,000 volunteers answered the call in the 1880s and 1890s.[5]

In the early 1930s, two young men from the Student Volunteer Movement began to challenge the status quo of mission thought with a new revelation. Cameron Townsend and Donald McGavran brought awareness to the fact that though churches had been established throughout the coasts and interior regions of the world, there were thousands of distinct language and people groups that would not be reached by the gospel because of cultural and linguistic isolation to those churches.[6] What began was the third wave of modern missions. It was the era of cross-cultural ministry and mission to the unreached people groups of the world. This also was met with opposition and took over forty years to take off. However, this period launched the most creative and fruitful era of church growth in history. This wave of mission emphasis, along with modern technology and global communication, has brought awareness to all the people groups of the world. Like the previous eras, it has been built on the backs of massive student mobilization and prayer initiatives.

A New Wave

It is in this third era that we find ourselves today. As we discussed earlier, while the revelation of missions was steered toward the remaining isolated unreached peoples, the world was experiencing the phenomenon of urbanization. As we began to realize the need to use the gospel as a bridge into isolated cultures and linguistic groups around the world, the Lord was bringing them out of isolation into our cities. I have argued that urbanization is being used by God to help us adequately reach the remaining unreached peoples of the world and bring this third wave of missions to completion.

However, would the mandate to make disciples of all nations be completed if we were to see the gospel simply preached or made available to every people group of the world? Will Jesus have adequately finished His goal to redeem the nations and buy back their kingdom expressions before God? As each new wave took us a step deeper into God's agenda in the nations, is there another step needed? What must happen to fulfill what Jesus spoke about in Matthew 24:14 when He declared that "this gospel of the kingdom will be preached in the whole world as a testimony to all nations," before the end would come?

Many are beginning to speak of a fourth wave. This wave would be earmarked by the discipling of the nations and teaching them to obey all that He commanded (28:20). According to some reports by Wycliffe Bible Translators, with new cooperation strategies, the Bible will have translation projects in place for the remaining known languages of the world in less than twenty years. What then? Are we done? If the goal of our Lord is to create a witness of His kingdom in each of the peoples of the world, what context is He bringing into existence that we must harness for that end? I suggest that God is urbanizing the planet in order for the church to both adequately complete the third era of modern mission and create the setting by which a fourth wave may occur.

When we consider the goal of discipling whole nations and distinct people groups, what do we really mean? Much of our worldview in Western Christianity has been a focus on the individual. We have developed scores of ministries and materials to restore, set free, and heal the individual through the work of Christ. However, do the purposes of God for the human story go beyond just the individual? Do corporate expressions of life have significance in the goal of reclaiming the image of God in man? If we step outside our Western individualistic orientation, we find that Scripture has much to say to corporate identities (maybe even more than it says to individuals). Granted, the individual has great importance to God. The fact that God has created every person who has ever lived uniquely and differently reveals the intimate and personal side of God. As a Father, He longs to relate to each of His children in personal and intimate ways. Yet, to see this as God's only agenda grossly underestimates His greatness and complexity.

The goal of restoring and healing the corporate expressions of the human story reveals the depth of which His image was truly inscribed in man. God is a Triune God. He is a God of both individual expression and corporate unity. By creating corporate life such as family, tribes, peoples, and nations, the Creator has built into mankind the context for a greater expression of His nature and character. Unless the Lord has, as a part of His redeeming agenda on the earth, a plan to restore in some way these corporate expressions, then He has not fully reclaimed His image in man. It should be our expectation to discover the ways in which God is moving history toward this goal. The mandate to instruct and immerse the nations into the person and ways of God is the culmination of that intent.

WHAT MOVES A NATION

Just as we saw in the other waves of modern mission, this fourth wave has been inspired by different prophetic voices. In 1975 God spoke to Loren Cunningham, Bill Bright, and other Christian leaders about seven spheres that influence all individual and corporate life. These included: family, education, government, media, arts, business, and technology. A recent book entitled *His Kingdom Come*, edited by Jim Stier, unveils numerous articles on the importance of each of the spheres and ways in which the body of Christ is beginning to engage them.[7] We teach these nation entities how to love their Creator by influencing the relational components that make up their corporate values and actions. However, it must be noted that if we are to influence these strategic spheres shaping nations then we must go to the cities. It is in the cities that these power structures are found. Furthermore, it is from the cities that the influence of these spheres is given voice.

We simply cannot seriously consider instructing and influencing the spheres making up a nation's values and character without engaging the cities in that nation which house those very institutions. When you think of the headquarters and trendsetters of each of these spheres, you quickly think of a city. We must become a part of the city, infecting all of its relational structures, if we are to see nations set free with the truth of who God is. Cities are evangelistic by nature. They are designed to market ideas. The city trains, equips, and sends ideas, culture, trends, and politics around the world.

John Dawson once said, "A nation is the sum of its cities."[8] What that means is that each city is like a child in a family. The direction of the family will be determined by the voice of these children and the alliances they make with each other. The dysfunction or health of the nation is determined by what is allowed to take place and be produced in its individual cities. If we win the war in these individual kingdoms, we win the war in the nation. What is needed is a new definition of missions. We must define the mission mandate not merely as a geographical engagement into another culture but the missional engagement into culture itself. God deserves a righteous expression through all spheres of interrelating. The authority and influence of these spheres exist for the purpose of furthering God's kingdom on the earth, not man's.

Perhaps you have a passion or vision for business, the arts, technology, education, or government. This new wave of missions will need another student mobilization movement able to integrate itself into that which God wants to redeem. As believers move into each of these spheres, influencing them with truth and righteousness, the effects will reach both nationally and internationally. We understand that a person cannot experience freedom, healing, and productive life without exploring the thoughts, actions, and emotions driving them. By influencing these aspects of a person's soul with truth, he or she is put on the path to wholeness and the life that God intended for them. We call this discipleship. What is needed is a corporate application to what we have done for years toward the individual. Yet how can we touch the soul of a nation without going to the heart? The heart of a nation, the central mechanism pumping all of a culture's values and trends in and out, is its cities.

THE CONTEXT FOR REVELATION

Perhaps even more significant than the authority and influence these spheres have on society is the power they have to actually reveal what God is like. More than just spheres of influence, they are spheres of revelation. Remember that God's goal is to create a witness of the good news of His kingdom in all nations before the end will come. A kingdom is the physical application of a king in relation to his subjects. In other words God desires to reveal to the nations what kind of King He is and how

His kingdom operates relationally to that which He has made. How then does God create that witness? The spheres mentioned above are relational institutions displaying unique relational influence. These then become a context by which we can display the nature and character of God, to draw the nations as a witness of the purposes they were created for.

The sphere of the family is an expression of unity in diversity and distinct functions serving each other in love and purpose. It shouts what God is like in the most basic and intimate expressions of our relational makeup. By influencing the family definition and structure in society, we create a stage by which a culture and nation can discover the father heart of God, His mothering care, and the way family members will serve each other for a greater good. Is it any wonder that this relational sphere in society is so fought over? Because all spheres in society are built on relationships, the health or dysfunction of the family sphere is the basic foundation for all the others.

How we function and facilitate education in a nation has the capacity to reveal who God is as well. Education, rightly understood, is the way by which we find feet to our pursuit of God, and the way we assimilate and wield that knowledge toward creating and co-laboring with him. By influencing education we have a context to reveal the order and majesty of God, and the loving assimilation of the two in regard to all that He has made. Education is no longer seen as simply a functional tool for the furtherance of our small dreams but a platform for discovering God and the bigness of His dreams.

All of us understand the authority government has to determine the direction of nations. Yet the importance of this sphere is not merely in wielding its power but in revealing the just, holy, and righteous ways of God. It's a context by which nations can discover how God governs and the fruit of righteousness in a land. Rather than simply arguing for the rightness of truth, we are given a relational kingdom context by which we can display the effects of justice and mercy working together for the good of a whole. Governments are judged or praised by the very standards our hearts tell us are right and just. When aspects of God's character and wisdom are seen in government, it will draw the nations, witnessing to the truth written in their hearts.

Media is a tool of communication. God is in fact the author of communication and the greatest, most creative communicator in the universe. Media is not something to be feared, but rather a platform to reveal the very origin of and the purpose for creative communication. As we enter the sphere of media, we are given the opportunity to show the world the loving commitment of a God who is not silent and has the capacity to speak and identify with us on a heart level. The arts are a platform to discover the beauty and complexity of God. They are able to reveal the ways His joy, celebration, and even pain are written into the fabric of the universe. The sphere of the arts is meant to be a bridge by which man can truly touch the very origin of beauty and imagination, which is God Himself.

Finally, business and technology are not only incredibly powerful tools within a culture but stages for revealing God as well. These spheres exist because God Himself is an inventor, creator, and entrepreneur. He is a God who labors with integrity and loving intent and rewards those who do the same. He has lovingly provided resources for man's use and is eager to co-labor with us in the assimilation and productivity of those resources. He is a loving Father who has provided the tools we need to love and care for all that He has made.

We have the opportunity, as God's children, to not merely wield these spheres for our own ends, but to enter them with the goal of displaying the greatness and beauty of God to a culture. It is through these interrelating spheres that we effectively immerse a nation in the person and character of God, and teach them to live out the truth of their design. Each sphere is either a megaphone for righteousness or the perversion of what is right. We understand that one of the first steps to deliverance in a person is to determine the wrong assumptions and conclusions driving their actions. Likewise a nation will only experience the redemption of their purpose in Christ as we enter the thought processes that are driving their actions. These foundational assumptions and values are rooted in the basic relational spheres that drive a nation. If we are to call a nation to repentance, it must be done on this level. We cannot repent of what we do not know is wrong, and we will not have a change of heart unless we see and have a revelation of what is right.

RECLAIMING OUR INHERITANCE

In the Gospel of Matthew, Jesus encourages His followers to understand the influence that God has given them. (See Matthew 5:13–16.) God's children are called to be the salt of the world. We are to effectively preserve that which is good and bring flavor to all aspects of life. He then makes a statement about the power of a city; it cannot be hidden.

The nature of community is that its voice is heard louder than the voices of its individual parts.

Driving down a highway at night, I can always tell when I am approaching a city. The sky lights up. There is usually an increase of traffic flowing in and out, and all of a sudden there are multiple radio stations that I can access for news or entertainment. I have never experienced the sensation of driving through a city without being aware of it; I've never driven through New York, Los Angeles, or Chicago and not known I had been there. Rather, we are usually all too aware, trying to navigate through the increased intensity of stimulus and activity. We actually build superhighways around cities so we don't have to interact with all the tension provided by these increased infrastructures of intense communal living.

However, the reference that Jesus makes about the city's influence is given not as a discouragement but an opportunity. He tells the disciples that just as we would not put a light under a bowl, God also intends that light be displayed. He then challenges His followers, "In the same way, let your light shine before men, that they may see your good deeds and praise your Father in heaven" (Matt. 5:16). This is our inheritance. Just as Jesus brought light into the world, so we have been called to do the same. How do we do this practically? How do we display the very nature and character of the Father through our actions in such a way that people will see it and praise God for who they see He is?

In this verse, Jesus gives us both the calling and its application. We effectively display God when we enter the components that make up the very intense expressions of community that cannot by ignored, namely the city. We cannot afford to give our inheritance to the world. We have been called to disciple the nations. Why then do we try to take the superhighways around the city to reach that end? If we allow the world to influence the seedbeds of all culture rooted in our cities then we have lost the battle. The city is a gift. It can be both the classroom for discovering who God is and a megaphone that will shout its revelation to the world.

The impact that believers can make on a nation when they engage its spheres of influence is phenomenal. Some of history's greatest examples include William Wilberforce and the Clapham Group of which he was a part. This group was made up of eleven influential believers in early nineteenth-century England. They represented positions in government, education, the church, and business. Through their influence they saw not only laws changed governing slavery but reform in business practices and working environments, help for refugees, and social changes in gambling and bullfighting. They effectively changed the morality of a culture.

Similarly, in the late nineteenth century, William and Catherine Booth showed the world what could be done when believers brought awareness and action to the plight of a city's poor and disenfranchised. By the end of his life, the Salvation Army he founded had been established in more than 16,000 centers globally, causing such reform socially, religiously, and legislatively, that his audience was sought by kings and presidents worldwide. What these examples show us is that when even a small number of believers enter the spheres of society with a witness of God's truth, it can bring great change.

Where are the Clapham Groups of today? How are

we empowering the army of believers that already exists within the spheres of our megacities with both vision and tools to reclaim a witness of God's image in the corporate expressions of humanity? Today's megacities dwarf what existed only fifty years ago. The gift of the city to create a platform for the discovery of truth and the voice to shout it to the world is greater now than ever before. If this fourth wave of missions—to see the nations and people groups of the world discipled—is to succeed, then we must go to the cities.

Our church planting and missionary endeavors must include strategies to facilitate this hidden army of believers existing in the spheres of our societies. These strategies should include not only the discipling of a kingdom vision for the spheres that believers are engaged in but also creative ways to build missional communities and support structures around them. The success of groups like the Clapham Society and Salvation Army was realized in part because of the way that they carried a corporate vision for change and built community around each other in that goal. Perhaps we need more church planting models that can exist and multiply, not separate from the spheres of society, but inside them. Perhaps mission organizations that train and mobilize missionaries need to not only train missionaries with a vision to enter the spheres of society, but also create missional communities and support networks that would identify them as true missionaries existing within the spheres of society, empowering them to succeed in their Great Commission calling.

Recently I was invited to a meeting of believers in an office located in the Chicago Board of Trade. This institution is one of the most influential trading entities in our country. All meat and grain from the U.S. that is traded anywhere in the world must go through the Board of Trade in Chicago. This institution exerts great power and influence but is also known for corruption and unjust practices. I sat in a room with about fifteen believers who work in this influential institution.

They meet a few times a week in the morning before the trading floor opens to discuss what the Scriptures have to say about righteous business practices and integrity, and to pray for each other's witness to the nonbelievers who they work with. They shared the struggles they faced as believers, experiencing persecution for their faith from their employers and fellow workers. They prayed earnestly for each other to remain strong and have the grace to fulfill God's call on their lives. They began the meeting by introducing one new believer who had recently received the Lord and one fellow worker who had come to hear more about being a follower of Jesus. I felt as if I was fellowshiping with believers in an underground church of some restricted nation. Their passion was real; they truly believed that God had brought them together as a community to display God's truth in that environment, and the way they built each other up in the faith was empowering.

After the meeting was over, one of the believers asked if I wanted to go with him to the trading floor. As we walked around the masses of people, busy trading millions of dollars' worth of commodities, he would introduce me to one believer after another and whisper to me the challenges they were facing by following Jesus in that environment. One had been demoted because his employer discovered that He was a passionate believer; another had been passed over for a promotion, which was rightfully his, because he had been witnessing to his employer and talking to him about some of the practices going on that lacked integrity. He pointed out one who was seeking and close to accepting Christ, one who they were praying would find Jesus, and one who had come to them for prayer because he was going through a difficult divorce.

Truly this is church at its best. Furthermore, I would suggest that it is the picture of the new church movement that God seeks to release in our day. Can we believe God for church planting movements that not only create a voice toward the spheres of culture, but a voice from within those very spheres of change? Are the "Simple Church" and "Organic Church" models that have arisen in the last couple decades actually a revelation from the Lord to equip us for a new mission field? Rather than simply being a reaction to institutional church, are these models being given to us so that we can actually enter territories that can truly disciple the nations and fulfill the Great Commission? Does this picture of church cause your heart to beat with excitement? Perhaps you were born for such a time as this. In the next section, we will look at how God intends to display His glory on the earth and how these new expressions of churches existing on every level of human relationship play a part in that goal.

PART 3
THE CITY, OUR WITNESS

For the earth will be filled with the knowledge of the glory of the LORD, *as the waters cover the sea.*
—HABAKKUK 2:14

Chapter 9
FILLING THE EARTH WITH HIS GLORY

*Arise, shine, for your light has come, and the glory
of the LORD rises upon you. See, darkness covers the
earth and thick darkness is over the peoples, but the
LORD rises upon you and his glory appears over you.*
—ISAIAH 60:1–2

*Neighborhoods are reached one person and family
at a time. Cities are reached one neighborhood at a
time. Nations are reached one city at a time. The
world will be reached one nation at a time.*
—JACK DENNISON[1]

I N THE FIRST two sections of this book, we discussed
how God is using urbanization to draw the nations of
the world together and reach them with the gospel in
ways we have never seen before. We saw how He may be
using the context of a city to draw out men's brokenness
so they may be healed. We also explored how the city is
the most adequate tool in the earth to effectively disciple
nations into their God-given purpose as corporate life. As
God's children it is imperative that we understand the
story He intended to write on the earth and what He is

doing through the ages to redeem and restore that original plan. We then judge those unique trends occurring in each generation as either a potential for furthering His goals or a hindrance to it. I have argued that the city defines our home, and what we were both designed for and are being prepared to live in for all of eternity. I have also displayed the gift that the city is to the church in world evangelism and the finishing of the Great Commission.

Urbanization may play an even deeper role in God's redeeming purposes for all that He has made, the chance to adequately display His glory and restore a witness of His image on the earth. In this chapter, we will take a deeper look into that possibility. In order to do so, we will need to take a look at the way God reveals truth in general. We will also need to take a journey through Scripture to see how His redeeming strategy is being woven throughout history. My hope is that this will not be cumbersome, but rather build an excitement in you for how the times in which we live play into that amazing story. I would submit to you that the way in which God is urbanizing the planet is bringing His purposes for man to completion, setting the stage for the return of Christ and preparation of His bride.

DISPLAYING HIS SPLENDOR

God is committed to restoring His purpose for man. Yet, since the fall of Adam and Eve, man has increasingly grown into deeper levels of darkness and an inability to adequately see truth. If God's goal for man is the restoration of relationship, He must remove the barriers to that relationship. The Scriptures are essentially a record of how the Lord is unfolding His original plan for the human story while removing the barriers to its relationship with Him.

The life, death, and resurrection of Jesus are the center of that redeeming story. He fulfilled what the several thousand years prior to His arrival were working toward and released the components needed to bring all things into restoration in the years that followed.

Jesus fulfilled God's ability to extend mercy toward our rebellion in the universe while remaining a just God who defends and protects truth. However, this could not automatically restore relationship with the nations He had formed. Mankind, with all of its individual and corporate expressions, could not enter that free gift of relationship unless God found a way to remove their blindness, reintroducing them to the One who both defined them and was worthy of their trust. If true relationship is to be restored, releasing the kind of trust that is needed for transformation to occur, then God must reveal His beauty and the trustworthiness of His character. This is not something we deserved, but still something that He, in His love, has been committed to. How then does God reveal Himself and reintroduce into the hearts and minds of the nations what we have been created for? For sure, this has been a part of His plan throughout history, and what will help us to understand what He is doing today.

The strategy we see God using in the Bible to fulfill the goal of restored relationship is something called the "display of His glory." The Scriptures speak often of the "glory of the Lord." We sing songs about the earth being "filled with His glory," or asking God to "show us His glory." The Psalmist sang in reference to God's glory and the need to sing of it to the nations. (See Psalms 57:5; 72:19; 96:3.) Moses pleaded with God to not send him to Pharaoh unless God show him His glory. (See Exodus 33:12–23.) The word literally shows up hundreds of times in the Old and New Testaments. However, what do we mean when we speak of His glory filling the earth? Why is it even necessary? It is an obvious thread throughout God's purposes, and yet, how do we perceive Him actually fulfilling that goal?

The Hebrew word for *glory* means visible weight or splendor.[2] By implication it is the physical, recognizable display of something's greatness. When we see a great athlete performing an amazing act of physical accomplishment, we say things like, he or she was in "their glory." It means, for that brief moment we were able to visibly see those aspects of who they were, which made them great and superior to others. This is how God has chosen to reveal truth in general. He wants all of creation to understand who He is and therefore understand who they are in relation to Him, being the One who is the foundational description of reality. When God made Adam and Eve in His image, it not only gave us the capacity to relate to Him, but it established a witness on the earth of what God looks and acts like as a standard for all of creation. When Adam and Eve chose to live independently of God, they not only severed their relationship with Him but also fell short of the glory of God (Rom. 3:23). The image of God in man had been marred. The display of God's splendor on the earth had now been made unclear and perverted. By Genesis chapter 6, we discover that man's heart had become so darkened to its original glory that "every inclination of the thoughts of his heart was only evil all the time" (v. 5).

God has chosen things throughout history to reveal His splendor and has promised that He would fill the earth with His glory, "as the waters cover the sea" (Hab. 2:14). God is a God of light and revelation (1 John 1:1–5). He seeks to display who He is in visible and tangible ways so that we might be drawn to Him and understand our design and purpose. All of redemptive history fits into God's goal of recreating a display of His image on the earth, effectively drawing the nations back into relationship with Him.

THE ERAS OF HIS GLORY

As we discussed in an earlier chapter, there have been eras of human history. We can now see how those eras were a part of God filling the earth with a visible and tangible witness of His character and splendor. First, God directs man to fill the earth so that the diversity of nations could develop and a context might be established for the complexity of who God is. Secondly, we see God choosing one nation to reveal His glory to the other nations, that they might be drawn to Him. (See Genesis 12:1–3; Isaiah 60:1–3.) This glory, or visible display of God's splendor, was revealed to the nations through the way that Israel related to God as a corporate entity. All other nations now had a chance to discover what God approves or disapproves of, and what His character was like in relationship to a nation. One nation was chosen to reveal God's faithfulness and holiness and give witness to the purposes He had for all nations.

Finally, we see God deciding once again to choose something that would further give witness to who He is and what He has intended for man. He chooses to place His name, or representation of His character, on a temple and on a kingdom expression called a city, Jerusalem (2 Chron. 6:5–6). During this period of history, God is seen fighting for and protecting these two expressions of His glory (Ps. 147:12–14; 1 Kings 11:10, 13). God declared to the world through the temple expression that He is a God who seeks to dwell with men. Furthermore, He sought to reveal to the world, through the kingdom expression of a city, the righteous way He governs in the affairs of men. God displayed incredible jealousy over the purity of His temple and the city Jerusalem because of the role they played as accurate witnesses of who He is to the rest of the nations. From this point on, God sends prophet after prophet to reveal His heart and purpose for these two entities. Much of the Old Testament is a display of blessing and judgment on the temple and Jerusalem, in a way that would protect the value of their witness. Finally God is seen rejecting the very things that He had chosen because they no longer displayed His glory accurately. (See Jeremiah 4:14, 8:5; 2 Kings 23:26–27.)

However, because it is God's intent to reveal Himself and what He has designed in a tangible way on the earth, He promises to restore the temple and Jerusalem, so His glory may once again be displayed (Isa. 31:5; 40:1–2; 52:9). After their captivity in Babylon, the people are led by Ezra to rebuild the temple. The people are then led by Nehemiah to rebuild the walls around Jerusalem, once again seeking to protect the vision God had to display His glory through her. The book of Haggai is God's prophetic word to the people as they seek to rebuild the temple. And finally, the book of Zechariah is God's prophetic vision for the restoration of the city of Jerusalem and all its glory. The Old Testament can be summed up as a record of God establishing the nations, the choosing of one nation to witness to the others about their intended relationship with their Maker, and the establishment of a temple and kingdom expression, revealing to those nations the way in which they would find their unique intimacy and purpose with the Lord.

It is at this point that Jesus enters history. Remember that Scripture says that at the "fullness of time," Christ came (Gal. 4:4, kjv). The Old Testament period of history was preparation for what Jesus would accomplish. It was a shadow of greater things and meant to point to what the Christ would bring about (Gal. 3:23–25; Heb. 10:1). The Gospel of Matthew, as the first book of the New Testament, appropriately begins with a genealogy so that we might understand how Jesus fit into the flow of God's redeeming story. The eras of that history are summed up in Matthew 1:17: "Thus there were fourteen generations in all from Abraham to David, fourteen from David to the exile to Babylon, and fourteen from the exile to the Christ." It is important to note the three significant points of redeeming history mentioned in this verse. Abraham represents the choosing of a nation for God's glory. The time of David represented the choosing of a temple and kingdom to display His splendor. The era following the Babylonian captivity displayed God's jealous purposes over those entities and His prophetic voice to one day reclaim their significance. Jesus then enters as the one who would give meaning and purpose to those previous eras as well as release a new era of the display of God's glory on the earth.

When Jesus entered Jerusalem in preparation for His death, He is seen doing two things. Consequently these two actions are the only time that we see Jesus showing great frustration. The first thing He does is enter the temple and violently chase out the moneylenders, declaring that His house was to be a house of prayer for all the nations. Secondly, while entering the city of Jerusalem He sees a fig tree without fruit and curses it, causing it to die. Can you see how this relates to what He had worked to accomplish in the nations up to this time? The two things that God chose to put His glory on are the two things that He shows jealousy over. God's heart is broken and frustrated by the inability of His temple to display to the nations His desire to dwell with them. Equally, He is frustrated that this kingdom expression called the city of Jerusalem had failed to bring forth the fruit of righteousness that He had designed it to do before the nations.

THE ERA OF HIS SON

The appearance of Jesus into human history catapulted God's agenda to fill the earth with His glory and reclaim His original intent of creating man in His image. First, Jesus is the very physical representation of who God is and how He operates within relationship to all that He created (Col. 1:15–20). The purpose of Jesus entering the world was to once and for all reveal the fullness of God's character in a tangible way and release the plan of God that would recreate His image in man. God put on flesh and we saw His glory (John 1:1–18). Never again would there have to be confusion about what God is like. Jesus revealed the Father's character, emotion, and sacrificial love in a visible and tangible way for every generation to see. God, through Christ's sacrifice and willingness to walk among us, removed the relational barriers that kept us from Him.

Through the first Adam, God initiated His purposes for mankind. However, it is in Christ, whom the Scriptures reveal as the second Adam, that God will fulfill those purposes (1 Cor. 15:45–49). What Jesus has done is buy back the temple expression and kingdom expression in the nations. He has in fact now made the two one. Revelation declares that He, after buying back the nations with His blood, has made them to be a kingdom and priests unto their God (Rev. 5:9–10). We are now the temple by which God's Spirit dwells and the expression of His kingdom on the earth (Eph. 2:22; Luke 17:20–21).

Jesus has made it possible to place His Spirit in those who receive Him, releasing His glory on the earth in ways that could not have been done previously. The mystery of God's accomplishment is that now we, who have Christ in us, are the "hope of glory" on the earth (Col. 1:26–27). Therefore we are called to be a witness to the nations of what His character is like, what He dwells with, and how He operates relationally with all that He has made (Acts 1:8). Just as He was the light that came into the world, we are now called to be His light and glory to the ends of the earth as His Spirit lives and moves in us. We are God's tools to fill the earth with the glory of the Lord as the waters cover the sea (Hab. 2:14). Jesus, after rising from the dead, tells His followers that just as the Father had sent Him into the world to display His glory, He now would send them to do the same (John 20:21).

It is God's agenda to bring all things to completion under Jesus (Col. 1:19–20). For the last two thousand years His followers have carried the light of who He is into the nations of the world. Yet, I would argue that in order to bring all things to the place where the followers of Jesus represented every "tribe and language and people and nation" (Rev. 5:9) as a unified bride for God's Son, God must create a context on earth by which that bride can be prepared and "beautifully dressed for her husband" (21:2). Furthermore, since God's strategy for attracting the nations to the truth is to visibly display an aspect of that truth, it must be the plan of God to create a stage by which the truth of what the nations were created for can be visibly seen. Unless history moves toward these two realities, we will not see the culmination of God's redeeming story written on the earth.

BRINGING IT TO COMPLETION

By urbanizing the planet, God has created the perfect context for the nations to be able to see the full glory of God and find a witness of the home they are being redeemed for. Never before in history has something existed that could adequately set the stage for God's presence to dwell with the nations in a unified way. If God's purpose is to reclaim His image in man, then never before have we had a context by which all the diversity of humanity could express itself in a sacrificial, loving, unified way that could shout the beauty of our triune God. God is a relater. We reveal what God is like on the earth by the way we relate according to His design in us.

Cities are community clusters interrelating geographically, socially, and functionally, kingdom expressions representing all the spheres of interrelating and how they either bless or exploit each other. God chose a kingdom expression in history for His glory, since He can only be visibly known through the right display of His design in these forms of interrelating. However, if that kingdom expression is still primarily a monoracial or monocultural expression, it is lacking in its ability to reveal all of God's character as a God of diversity in unity. Therefore, what God began to do in the nation of Israel must by necessity move toward a greater level of cultural, ethnic, and relational diversity if it is to adequately display the fullness of God's glory

What God did in the Old Testament was simply a shadow of what He intended to do through Christ after the fullness of the nations had been developed. God is now moving the diversity of humanity back together into geographical proximity where they might discover who God is through the interrelating of their diversity. The modern megacity could be defined simply as a multitude of interrelating community clusters. Multiple communities, representing all forms of diversity economically, generationally, racially, and culturally, can now relate to each other through the character of God and display who He is in an unprecedented way.

All of the cities' problems are relational problems. Those problems represent a complexity that has never been seen before. They represent a challenge to the gospel. If the life of Jesus and His gospel of the kingdom are accurate descriptions of reality, then they must work in these complex relational environments. If His kingdom cannot function in the city, it cannot be truth and no longer holds hope for the nations. Urbanization has given the church a chance to put God on display in ways we never could before. Yet, if we do not allow Jesus, through us, to walk among these relational complexities, then the world will not only distrust the validity of our message, but be robbed of the chance to see the full glory of God.

The city, when discipled and experiencing transformation in Christ, has by its very nature the ability to be the greatest witness of God's glory on the earth. The church needs the city, with all of its diverse interrelating complexities, to adequately reveal who God is to the nations. Furthermore, it is the modern city that has the capacity to display what the nations have been created for. However, this truth will only be realized when the city experiences a visible transformation, occurring when God's Spirit enters these complex, diverse, and challenging clusters of community interaction.

As God's people, we must go to the city because it is the place where truth is being defined and revealed. The Lord has set the stage for the display of His splendor. The nations are watching in search of hope and definition. It is time for us to shine!

Glory in Action

The greatness of who God is cannot be written on paper but on the lives of men. The world must be filled with a witness of that greatness if the nations are to be drawn to their Maker. God told the children of Israel that the result of His glory being put on them was that the nations would be drawn to their "light" (Isa. 60:1–3). This has always been God's strategy to reveal truth and effectively draw the nations of the world back into relationship with Him. The city is a gift to the purposes of God's people because it sets the stage for the display of His splendor. Not only does the city give us the most adequate context for the fullness of God's character to be seen in all of its relational complexity, but the activity and influence of the city is also a megaphone. Its voice cannot be hidden and therefore begs the question, What are the cities preaching to the nations?

Right now I am sitting at a small neighborhood coffee shop looking out onto a busy street, surrounded by diverse apartment buildings and businesses. There is a homeless man asking for help on the corner, being judged, ignored, or pitied by those who walk by. The buildings around me are filled with predominately single-parent homes, created through the breakup of the family in my culture. Their kids are walking to school, not sure if the brokenness in their home life is really an abnormal picture of what they were created for, since most of their friends are experiencing the same reality. There are a few homosexual couples sitting in the tables next to me, representing one aspect of the sexually broken people that make up the community here. A few of the businesses within view are closed down because of the financial struggles that tend to face the entrepreneurial spirit in the city. I can see other business owners working in their shops or looking out their windows with that familiar look of anxiety, wondering if they will survive, and what their life might be like if they do not.

There is an elderly woman and younger man out my window, both walking their dogs, the elderly woman asking the younger man a question. A cluster of people from different nationalities are getting on the bus in front of me, another half dozen starting to gather for the next one arriving in a couple of minutes. Some look stressed, others occupied with life. A crippled woman just walked by. Two guys are washing windows of one of the businesses. There are dozens of people walking the streets; old, young, wealthy-looking, those who are poor; a mentally ill man talking to himself; Chinese, Korean, Hispanic, African-American, Indian, and Middle Eastern; most not talking to each other or recognizing the richness of diversity walking past them. All around me and my little coffee shop is a sea of humanity. This is my coffee shop, my neighborhood, my neighbors: *my* gift, and *my* responsibility.

For some reason the scripture in Matthew 9:35–38 is going through my mind. When Jesus saw the crowds, "He had compassion on them, because they were harassed and helpless, like sheep without a shepherd" (v. 36). God longs to shepherd the complexity of people's lives in the city.

The street corner I just described is one of thousands just like it. There are seventy-seven different neighborhoods in Chicago's city limits. The average city block has two thousand people living on it, and in many neighborhoods you will find nearly two thousand people in each apartment building. The wealthy live right next to extreme poverty. Nations at war with each other around the world are not only in the same neighborhood in my city, but often live next to each other in the same apartment building. Markets cater to the masses with dozens of nationalities coming in contact with each other daily. Right now in Chicago's eighty-seven colleges and universities, young men and women are debating life, reality, and the pursuit of a productive existence. All of these social institutions of interrelating and shared life are stages by which men are meant to find God. We as His people are the players on that stage.

Every building, every block, every neighborhood is our church. The challenge to church planting today is not financial, but incarnational. We don't have to find a way to build our own gathering points; we simply need to enter what already exists. If God has given you a heart to pastor people, then perhaps a multiunit apartment building is your congregation. If you have been gifted with an entrepreneurial spirit and love for business, then a corporate office building or a street filled with dozens of family-owned businesses might be your parish. If you're a teacher, then the city is the most dynamic classroom that you could ever be given, made up of diverse students asking the most complex questions known to man. If you're an artist, why limit your vision to capture beauty on canvases? Make people your canvas and put the image of God on display. It will be a studio that nations, kings, and dignitaries will be drawn to.

Over the last twenty years in Chicago, I have learned of, and partnered with, many examples of the church living and impacting diverse community. Two recently published books that chronicle many of these stories are John Fuder's *A Heart for the City* and *A Heart for the Community*, edited by John Fuder and Noel Castellanos. When the church does what it was created to do, displaying God's character and ability to transform lives, the world takes notice. It is these pastors and church leaders, effecting change in the city, who are being asked to chair mayoral committees addressing the difficulties of city life. It is the church that has the capacity to heal, restore, and bring productivity to diverse communities. Often the leadership of our cities is not at odds with us when we do what we were created to do. We simply need to put truth on display, and the city will ask the church for help to do what they have given up hope on and lost meaning for.

I know of pastors whose phone numbers are on police commissioners' cell phone speed dials, called in when violence is escalating or when healing needs to happen in a neighborhood tragedy. One pastor told me of a one hundred-year-old neighborhood bank forgiving a three million dollar church debt simply because they recognized that it was the community efforts of their church, in one of the worst neighborhoods of the city, that have increased all of the bank's investment values. This bank, having never forgiven any debt for anyone before, forgave the church's debt on one condition: that they promised to continue transforming the neighborhood. Crime is being reduced, poverty cycles are broken over families, reconciliation is happening in segregated communities, and increased neighborhood productivity is being created not by increased government programs but the relational involvement of people who carry the principles of God's truth and character into the complexity of the city.

What remains, however, is the reality that these examples are still too few to address the growing needs of urbanization. Like Jesus' response to the crowds, we too need to cry out to "the Lord of the harvest to out send laborers into His harvest" field (Matt. 9:38, NJKV). The stage has been set in history for the full display of God's splendor. The nations are waiting for us to write the story of God's greatness, not in books but on the lives of men. The most complex, diverse, and relationally challenging communities of our world are the very places that God deserves to be seen in. We do not have to take God to the city. Yet it will only be when His people decide to move there that the world will discover He has been there all along.

Chapter 10
THE SECRETS OF THE KINGDOM

Wisdom cries aloud in the street, in the markets she raises her voice; at the head of the noisy streets she cries out; at the entrance of the city gates she speaks.
—**Proverbs 1:20–21, esv**

*Transformation is an **inside-out** and **downside-up** process. It is about reaching a critical mass of believers who are so empowered by the gospel of Christ that they change everything they touch—family, workplace, schools, business.*
—**Jim Herrington**[1]

DRIVING INTO THE city for the first time, our team of eleven was full of excitement. We had trained and prayed together for months, and now we were approaching Chicago with vision and dreams of what the Lord was going to do in our new home. We had been driving all night and woke early to see the sunrise coming over the skyline that ran along the enormous Lake Michigan. As we drove over the Chicago River Bridge, the car was silent. The city was huge! There were hundreds of high-rise office and apartment buildings. The freeway was beginning to fill up with the early morning rush of millions going to work.

I could sense everyone was feeling the same thing. The question going through all of our minds was, "What are we thinking?" The city was overwhelming! We felt small and powerless. I knew that we were not the only believers in the city, and yet I wondered in my heart if we had been presumptuous. Is it realistic to think that the followers of Jesus in Chicago, representing what I knew to be a small minority, could in fact redeem and restore God's purposes for a city of seven million people?

In the coming months and years, I struggled with that question often. I became increasingly convinced that urbanization taking place globally was playing into God's purposes for the nations. I also began to discover that God had in fact thought through how to accomplish His plan, and had not left His church without the tools needed to fulfill it. As I linked arms with believers throughout my city and watched the way they were affecting their communities I discovered what may be one of the best-kept secrets in much of the body of Christ: there is an enormous power in the way God's kingdom works.

Jesus told His disciples in Matthew 13 that the secrets of the kingdom of heaven have been given to His followers. He then tells them a story about how the message of the kingdom is sown into people's hearts; some have it stolen or choked out, and some receive it in such a way that they produce a crop, yielding "a hundred, sixty or thirty times what was sown" (v. 8). Much focus has been given in this parable about the type of hearts receiving the message. However, it would seem that the importance of the story is to encourage His followers that the message of the kingdom, or the way God operates with His subjects, has the ability to produce a large amount of fruit when it is received. What follow this encouragement are three sets of parables that reveal the way God's kingdom operates, influencing everything around it.

SECRETS REVEALED

Jesus begins and ends these parables with a set of stories emphasizing the same principle. The first story is about a man who sows good seed into his field only to discover that an enemy has sown weeds into that same field. The workers ask the master if they should tear out the weeds and the master says no, "let them both grow together" (Matt. 13:30). The danger is that if you uproot the weeds you may uproot the wheat as well. The master does not seem to be worried or discouraged about the effect this will have on the wheat. He assures his workers that they will be duly separated at the harvest. There is an enormous key in this story to both how God operates and the way that His harvest develops.

It was nine o'clock at night and a few of us pulled our van to the side of a street at a busy intersection in one of Chicago's notoriously violent neighborhoods. Only seconds after we unloaded, a police car swerved into the oncoming traffic lanes, sirens blaring, and pulled up next to our team. An officer rolled his window down and yelled at us, "What are you guys doing here?" I guess we looked a little out of place. I pointed across the street to where a small group of people had gathered from a nearby church and told the officer that we were here to meet up with the bishop and pray for the neighborhood. He understood but shook his head and simply told us to be careful, reminding us that this was not a safe area. We went across the street and hugged our friends, laughing about what had happened. For the next two hours I counted dozens of police cars, arriving nearly every three to five minutes, stopping around our intersection to handcuff or run off gangbangers and drug dealers. We heard gunshots periodically coming from somewhere, followed by more sirens.

The contrast between what was going on around us and what was happening on our corner was almost surreal. Our small group of ten to twelve believers sang worship songs and prayed for people walking by. No one seemed to mind the commotion going on around us as they responded to our encouragement and asked us to pray for different needs in their lives. Two ladies looked like they were headed to sell their bodies on the street, but lingered to hang out with our group and be ministered to by one of the neighborhood pastors. Two people who stopped decided to give their lives to Jesus. Before we left, we all had Communion,

- on a street corner,
- in a violent and broken neighborhood,
- in the sight of broken people,
- with Jesus.

Jesus said that the harvest field is the world, and the key to the kingdom of heaven is to let the "sons of the kingdom" remain together with the "sons of the evil one" (Matt. 13:38). The parallel passage in Luke's Gospel states that after giving the parable of the sower, Jesus declared that no one lights a lamp and puts it under a bowl, for "there is nothing hidden that will not be disclosed" (Luke 8:16–17). We are reminded that it is God's agenda to put His people and His presence with them on display. Why do we insist that the activities of worship and communion with our God be limited to safe and insulated environments? Have we limited the effectiveness of God's kingdom in the nations by doing so?

After stopping a woman in a downtown plaza to ask her if I could pray for her about anything, I was shocked by her response. She was genuinely struck by the offer, and told me that she had never tried to talk to God and didn't know how to do so. She then asked, however, if we needed to go somewhere or enter some church to pray since she was a little busy and didn't have the time. What puts that into people's minds? Have we so isolated our fellowship with God that people no longer understand that fellowship is to be a normal part of everyday life?

We must let the sons of the kingdom remain with the sons of the evil one if the secret of the kingdom's effectiveness is to be put into action. How visible are our relationship with and worship of our Maker to the rest of society? Is there anything that we do as believers in our church buildings that we cannot do with our neighbors in our apartment buildings, with workers at our favorite eateries, in the parks and plazas, or while riding on city buses? The key to the kingdom's power is in keeping it visible. It is not our religious activities that will impress people, but the way our relationship with God and the expectation of His presence in our lives affect our daily activities.

Consequently, since the churches in that violent neighborhood began to occupy the most crime-infested intersections of their community, the crime index has drastically changed. Bishop Peecher actually went to his police chief and asked him which were the worst intersections of the neighborhood, those which experienced the most homicides and violent crime. He then began to rally the churches to occupy those very spots during the time of week when most crime occurred. The Lord spoke to him one day and told him that the effectiveness of the church is not in how it yells at violence, but rather in its ability to create peace. So, they decided to take over these broken and violent areas by visibly being the church. After only a couple of months, the police chief told Bishop Peecher that the crime index—indicators influenced by all levels of violent crime and destructive behavior—in that spot had dropped, making one of the worst areas in the city statistically safer than most suburban communities.

Are we aware of this as the church? How has this been kept a secret from us? A small group of believers, who simply made their faith and relationship with God public in a geographic spot, were able to do what a city police force with millions of dollars of city budget could not. The police chief asked this pastor to come and meet with his department and explain to them what the secret was. The pastor simply told them that they went to the troubled area, prayed, worshiped, and had communion. The police chief did not believe him. After asking him the same question a few times and getting the same answer, the chief simply shook his head. He then encouraged Bishop Peecher that whatever it was he was doing, to somehow duplicate this in all the other troubled areas of the city.

Jesus said that where two or more are gathered in His name, He is there also (Matt. 18:20). Have we lost the geographic significance of this promise? The statement was made in reference to how the church was equipped to bind up darkness and loose God's kingdom on the earth. We have the ability to bring the One who spoke the worlds into existence into the darkest, most complex environments of the world. The *key is* to simply gather, in His name, in that geography. This is a secret that must not remain hidden any longer if we are to see God's glory fill the earth.

THE BASIS OF OUR CONFIDENCE

Following this first parable of the kingdom, Jesus then gives His disciples two parables that reveal the secret of the kingdom's influence. First He tells them that God's kingdom is like a mustard seed. Even though it is the smallest of garden seeds it produces the largest tree, drawing even the birds to make their nests in it (Matt. 13:31–32). When the principles of God's kingdom operate in a culture or community, though often small and sometimes unnoticed by more visible voices, it has the power to become the most influential. In his book *City Reaching*, Jack Dennison does a fantastic job presenting the influence that a "saturation" strategy can have in a city. He speaks of examples where a critical mass for city transformation can be reached sometimes with as little as 20 to 25 percent of a city's population living out their faith in Jesus in an intentional and integrated way.[2]

When my kids were young we had to find creative outlets for activity. Since most who live in the city do not have the luxury of backyards, we went to the neighborhood play lots or local play places. Since my wife often took the night shift with the kids, my duty consisted of taking the kids out to play in the mornings so she could catch up on sleep. Whether I wanted it to or not, our life as a family became visible to all the other moms and dads in the community. How absolutely refreshing and fulfilling this was! Sharing life with others became so easy in this context. I almost wish my kids were young again so I could avail myself of the incredible evangelistic gift they were to me. The enemy wins a great victory by convincing us that what is best for our children is to somehow insulate and isolate them from the rest of the world. My kids are now teenagers and already have developed such a rich worldview and experienced the joy of impacting others' lives in ways that most adults have never experienced.

One morning my kids and I went to a nearby play place. My kids are very close, but as often occurs, something led to a disagreement, which led to a fight, which led to someone getting his or her feelings hurt. I heard their voices get loud among the other kids on the playground, and looked up to see them running toward me, each with a cry for justice. I didn't realize how many moms and other children were watching us.

We simply handled it the way we always did. I had each share his or her side of the story. I then told them how only through forgiveness could we have relationship and be healed. I asked one if they wanted to say they were sorry and ask for forgiveness, and they did. I then asked the other if they were willing to forgive. I told them that if they didn't forgive, the other one couldn't experience freedom. They said they wanted that, so forgiveness was communicated. They then turned around and ran off together like they were best friends again.

I just went back to reading. However, a few minutes later a mom came over and said that she had been watching how I handled the situation. She then thanked me for displaying such an amazing way of teaching my kids about relationship. I didn't think anything of it, but to her it was like a breath of fresh air and encouragement. When we live out the principles of God's kingdom in a community it brings life and hope to those who see it.

Jesus said that the fruit of His kingdom would grow to be the largest, most attractive tree in the garden, so that even the birds looking for somewhere to rest will build their nests in it. Can you see the power of God's kingdom lived out in proximity to the world? People are flying around like restless birds looking for something to put their hope in, something that they can build their life on. If we do not allow ourselves to be physically planted in the midst of the world, we cannot provide this effect.

Recently I was at my neighborhood grocery store. I was paying for my groceries and the cashier asked me how my kids were? He said, "You have a daughter who is probably about sixteen now and a son who is probably about thirteen, right?" I had seen this guy for years coming to this store, but I was still impressed at how good his memory was. He told me how he remembered me always carrying my son on my arm when he was just a toddler. We laughed about how he was practically another limb on my body for the first three years of his life. He then looked at me seriously and said, "You know, I remember something that happened years ago that I have never forgotten." He told me how when my kids were little, and my son was still a toddler, he was gathering carts in the lot one day and saw me getting my kids out of our car. My son was throwing a temper tantrum about something, and as I was holding him in my arms, he just reeled back and slugged me in the face. He said that he stopped and watched, because he was curious to see what I would do. I do not remember this event, of course, but he said that I did not get angry or lash back; I simply turned around and got back into the car, and then we got out a few minutes later with my son smiling and everything seem-ingly all right. What he said next shocked me. He said, "I have never forgotten that day. I stood there amazed at what

I saw because I had never seen a father handle it that way. It made a deep impression on me."

We as the church often struggle trying to find ways to get our message heard by the world. We spend millions of dollars on creative ways to get the message out. What would happen, however, if we simply located ourselves in such proximity to the world that they would see our message lived out? This man was now approaching me relationally because of seeing something displayed about fatherhood that he had never experienced in sixty years of his life. I am convinced that critical mass is reached in cultural transformation not by the point at which our voice reaches a certain level of magnification, but when our lives reach a certain level of community integration. People are hungry. When you set a feast before them long enough, when they are close enough to smell its aroma, they will eventually come to the table.

THE KEY IS INTEGRATION

Jesus follows the example of the mustard seed with a parallel story about how the kingdom of heaven is like a leaven that a woman mixes (hides or incorporates[3]) into a large amount of flour until the whole loaf is leavened. The *Webster's 1828 Dictionary* defines *leaven* as anything that makes a general change in the mass.[4] The person of Jesus and the principles of His kingdom are like leaven. They are a living entity with the ability to change what it comes in contact with on a cellular level. The key to its effectiveness is in the way it is worked into and throughout the substance it comes in contact with. Jesus was giving us the secret to our ability to change society and ultimately disciple the nations. We must be applied into that society and culture, worked into all aspects of its interrelating, in order to affect change on a cellular level. The dough is lifeless. It's the yeast that is a living fungus with the ability to mass-produce and multiply throughout the dough, bringing life into its otherwise lifeless state.

Does this encourage you? As an urban generation, you have been given the greatest context to display the truth of who God is and the application of His healing to the nations. We simply must embrace the key to what makes God's kingdom effective. We need to empower the believers who already exist in the city, as well as call a movement of believers into the cities, with a vision of what can be accomplished if they allow themselves to relationally integrate into all the spheres of community and culture. It simply cannot be done any other way. We will not effectively change the nations by speaking at them from safe and isolated environments. Jesus modeled the way of His kingdom when He left heaven, became one of us, and walked with us in such a way that we saw His glory (John 1:14).

Chicagoans look forward to spring and summer. After enduring several months of bitter cold, the warm weather brings life to the city. The ten miles of lakefront parks stretched across the city attract tens of thousands on the weekends. Hardly a square yard of these parks is not covered with some cookout or sports activity. As a team we love this time of year because it is so easy to interact with the people of our community. Normally, we have regular weekly cookouts where we set up a couple of grills and cook two to three hundred hot dogs for anyone who comes by. Often churches in the area help us with this. It's a great time to fellowship and enjoy our neighbors.

Recently, we had one of our regular cookouts and a

team of Chinese young people came to help us from a Chinese church in Chicago. Like always, hundreds of people would stop for a hot dog and talk with our team. There are usually people from dozens of different nationalities. It's a genuinely good time of hanging out with the diversity of our neighborhood, and always includes team members praying for people and encouraging them in the Lord. After being there for nearly two hours, we began to clean up, and a man came over to me. He was an African-American man from the neighborhood. He said he had been sitting on his car and watching us for almost the entire time we had been there. He said that we caught his attention because we represented so much diversity, and he genuinely wanted to know what we were doing. He told me how he was amazed that we actually looked like we were enjoying ourselves as well as those who came by to hang out with us. He looked at me with all seriousness and said, "I have lived in Chicago my whole life and what I have seen today has truly given me hope." He asked who we were and why we were doing what we did. I told him that I lived in the neighborhood as well, and shared with him the vision that the Lord had for the nations and what He was able to do in our lives.

God wants to put His kingdom on display. When we allow that to happen, it brings life into whatever it comes in contact with. I find it interesting that Jesus used the word for *hid* when describing how the leaven would be applied. We do not need to announce our entrance into society or make a noise about our presence. The key to the kingdom is the way that it is often quietly incorporated into the daily life of a community or sphere of society. Its effectiveness once again is not in being the largest or loudest seed in the garden, but rather the one that has the capacity to mass-reproduce and bud into all corners of that environment.

Ten years ago we purchased a small apartment building as a place to house interns and volunteer workers. My family lived on the first floor. We had only lived there for a year or two before a man came knocking on my door. He introduced himself and said that he lived down the street. He said that we had never met, but that he had watched the people living in our building for some time. He saw the way that we interacted with the neighbors and community and knew that we must be good people. He apologized for bothering me, but told me that he was going through a hard time with his wife and child and did not know whom to turn to. He just thought if there was anyone he could trust it would probably be someone in our building.

These stories are not meant to build up me or any member of our faith community, but rather to give examples of how impacting God's kingdom can be when it becomes visible and integrated into the brokenness of the world. It is time to let this secret out. This urban generation is gifted and attracted to community. There is a trend in this millennial generation to move back into intense and diverse community life. We need to give that desire purpose and empower the followers of Jesus with the secrets of His kingdom. I trust the Lord for a new movement of believers to arise; one that integrates into society rather than find ways to separate from it; one that will live out the principles of God's kingdom with such visibility and proximity to the human story that it will effectively put God on display and change that story into His.

OWNING THE KINGDOM

Finally, the last parables the Lord gives His disciples concerning the keys to His kingdom's effectiveness were stories about men who sold everything they had to purchase it (Matt. 13:44–46). The first story is about a man who, after discovering the treasure that is God's kingdom, sells everything he has to buy the field it is in. The second story is about how the kingdom operates. Jesus says that the kingdom of heaven is like a man looking for fine pearls, who after finding one, sells all he has to buy it. The way God's kingdom works is by searching out that which is most valuable and then selling all we have to get it. This passage has been used often to teach us the value of giving up all we have to obtain Jesus in our lives. However, I would suggest that its application in the context in which it is given is meant to convince us to search out that which will most effectively release the fruitfulness of God's kingdom and to encourage us to sell all we have to own it when it is found. Not only are there secrets to the effectiveness of God's kingdom, but also in order to obtain those secrets, we must be willing to own them, though they cost us all we have.

The greatest example to this kingdom principle is the incarnation of Christ. According to *Webster's 1828 Dictionary*, the word *incarnation* means "the act of assuming flesh, or of taking a human body and the nature of man."[5] In other words, Jesus did not only come to Earth, but also took on the nature, temptations, and surroundings of the environment He entered. This cost him something. Paul describes what Jesus gave up and left behind in his letter to the Philippians (2:5–11). He reminds us that, though Jesus had all the rights of divinity and heaven, He was willing to give it all up to reveal God to man. He then tells us that our "attitude should be the same as that of Christ Jesus." Jesus told His disciples, "As the Father has sent me, I am sending you" (John 20:21). What does this mean for His followers? Is there a principle outlined for us through these passages that reveals the secret of God's kingdom effectiveness?

There is a treasure hidden in the city. The bottom line, however, is that we cannot enjoy that treasure by simply renting the field. We must own the field. We must make the city our home, effectively clothing ourselves with the city's nature, temptations, and the struggle of its surroundings. This may cost us everything. In order to release the effectiveness of God's kingdom on earth, God put on the flesh of that earth and changed it from the inside out. If we are to disciple nations, recognizing the significance that the modern city now holds in that process, we will need to become an urban dweller. All of the city's diverse communities and interrelating spheres of influence are worlds in which God's Spirit desires to be fleshed out. We are now the body of Christ. The principle of how God displays truth and touches the brokenness of humanity is still the same. The grace and truth of God must be clothed, that it might visibly walk into the lifeless human story, giving it life once again.

All of us who are longing to give the Lord what He is worthy of in the nations are like that man searching for fine pearls. The activity of the church in every generation has been to search out that which will most effectively release the power of God's kingdom in that age. It is the glory of every generation that once it has discovered its miracle for the multiplication of God's kingdom in that age, it would be willing to sell all it has to obtain it. I have argued in this book that the way that God is urbanizing the world is in fact a miraculous gift to His church. Yet we cannot harness its potential unless we are willing to permeate it with our lives. Though we must continue to mobilize God's people into every geographical location where people exist, we can no longer ignore the city. Notwithstanding the gift that the city is to the purposes of God on the earth, we will need a movement of believers who are willing to clothe themselves in urban life if we are to simply keep up with the phenomenal migration happening globally toward the city.

The call to the city is no longer for those who already see the city as home, but also for those willing to trade their former home for a new one. The call is not only for those who already identify with the nature of urban life but for those who are willing to clothe themselves in a new nature, in hopes of harnessing the gift that is the city. The call is being given to a generation not satisfied with finding a way to simply tolerate the city, but rather willing to make the city's struggles and blessings its own in order to serve God's purposes in the human story. As the first urban generation in human history, what will you do with that distinction?

CONCLUSION

HAVE YOU EVER wondered what it must have been like to be a part of that small team of twelve men sent out by the nation of Israel to spy out the Promised Land? Imagine the excitement they must have felt to be the first to lay eyes on the territory that God had promised them. God had spoken to them of a land that would be full of fruitfulness and purpose. Numbers 13 and 14 record the story. We are told that they walked the length and breadth of the land. The fruit was so great that they had to break off a branch full of grapes just to take it back with them lest no one believe their testimony. At first they record the land as the very thing God had promised. But then it happened; they saw giants in the land and large fortified cities. Their hearts melted. All of a sudden the team was divided. Ten men are greatly discouraged and conclude that though this is in fact a good land, its challenges are insurmountable.

The testimony they give to the rest of the Israelites produces great distress. The Scriptures say that the whole community raises their voices and weep aloud. However, Joshua and Caleb stand up and try to embolden the children of Israel. They declare that the land is exceedingly good and that they should go up and take it, that they need not be afraid of the giants or fortified cities because the Lord will surely give it to them. Yet it was not enough, and a generation missed the opportunity to fulfill God's purposes through them. Consequently, when another generation comes of age, they rise to the challenge and are led by Joshua and Caleb, who are now in their eighties, to indeed take the territory God promised and display His glory to the nations surrounding them.

Two thousand years ago, Jesus told His followers to go into all the world and disciple all nations. They were given the mandate to display the gospel of His kingdom as a witness to those nations in preparation for His return. Jesus has been effectively going before His followers in every generation to pave the way for the success of that mission. Laid out before every generation are territories and "miracles" of His design. These new advancements to the kingdom of God throughout the ages are unique to the unfolding of God's redemptive purpose on the earth, and specifically prepared for the calling He has given His children to display His greatness to the nations. It is our responsibility to recognize the territory He wants to give us and face the giants of those new frontiers with faith and courage. The urbanization of the planet and the modern city is a "good land." It is filled with fruitfulness and purpose in the story that God is writing on the earth. What is needed is a generation to arise that will enter the urban world and harness its gift for God.

Mankind started in a garden but will end in a city. It was God's agenda to fill the earth and effectively create diversity in the human story. Once developed, that diversity could then be brought back together in a type of diverse unified relational expression that could reclaim His image in man. We are experiencing the era of human history that is the great return of the diversity of the world into geographical and relational proximity, setting the stage for the preparation of a corporate entity of diversity in unity that God will both marry and dwell with for all of eternity. The city is a glimpse of what we are being redeemed for.

Global urbanization is bringing the unreached, isolated peoples of the world into reachable environments. The modern city gives the church not only the proximity to the unreached but the ability to provide resources, train, and facilitate the gifts of those distinct peoples back around the world. The city is setting the stage for the development of the greatest missionary force every released upon the world, a missions movement made up of the diversity of the nations and people who can identify with all the brokenness of the human story.

The urban dweller lives in a hothouse environment by which all insecurity, fear, and relational brokenness is forced to the surface. God is effectively bringing all of the brokenness of the human story out in the open so that it must be dealt with. The church was designed to live in this environment. If God's people will move into the cities of the world, they will touch men's brokenness and become God's healing agent to the nations. The city is a gift to the people of God. Every sphere of influence and interrelating is found in the city. If we infect these spheres from the inside out, we can fulfill God's mandate to disciple and immerse the nations of the world into His presence and character.

For the first time in history, we have a context by which the fullness of God's greatness and splendor can be seen in every expression of diversity in the human story. When God's people bring a witness of who He is in that relational context of diversity ethnically, generationally, economically, and functionally, the earth will be effectively "filled with His glory as the waters cover the sea." As those who carry the mandate to display the fleshed-out glory of God before the nations, we need the city. If our calling is to display God's greatness, rather than just speak of it, then we need the city. If we are to be given access to the unreached peoples of the world, we need the city. If we are to harness the secrets of God's kingdom to effect change on a cellular level in the soul of a nation, it is to the heart of the nations, its cities, we must go.

I have spent the last twenty years in an environment I would have never chosen for my family or myself. I have walked and touched the city and have discovered that it is truly a "good land" for God's people to be. I have worked alongside and heard the reports of many others co-laboring in my city as well as around the world, and have heard the same: it is a "good land" for the people of God. The world is urbanizing at a faster rate than any country has been prepared for. With that phenomenal migration of all the world's diverse, complex, and struggling peoples into cities has come great challenges. Yet, is it possible that this has served the purposes of God in the nations and equipped His people with the power to fulfill their honor of extending His kingdom to all peoples?

I would submit to you that the urbanization of the planet is the culmination of God's redeeming purposes for man. As the first urban generation in human history how will you embrace the city? As expressions of church and mission in the twenty-first century, what adjustments might we have to make to reveal who God is to an urban world? How can we effectively train this urban generation to know and experience God amidst the noise and stress of an urban environment? What must we speak to the city to call forth its greatness and purpose for God? The enemy has kept the treasure of the city buried and hidden from God's people for too long.

Finally, after twenty years, I am more convinced than ever that God *does* in fact live in the city. He is attracted to the city because it is the place where man can find God and experience His dwelling among the nations. Perhaps like me, you have heard Him say to your heart, "Will you come and live in the city with Me?" Jesus told us, "The kingdom of heaven is like treasure hidden in a field. When a man found it, he hid it again, and then in his joy went and sold all he had and bought that field" (Matt. 13:44). It's time for the people of God to buy the field, with great joy!

Appendix

AN URBAN WORLDVIEW
AND ITS IMPLICATIONS FOR
CHURCH AND MISSIONS

A s WE HAVE discussed in this book, in the last fifty years the world has seen a historical shift from a predominately global rural culture to an urban existence. In 1950 the world was only 29 percent urbanized. Today over 50 percent of the world lives in cities, creating the first urban generation in history. At the current rate, the world will be 90 percent urban by the end of the century.

The twentieth century was a story of urbanization in North America and Europe. The twenty-first century will be remembered as the urbanization of the Eastern Hemisphere and the developing world. North America has led the world in urbanization over the last fifty years, from 64 percent in 1950 to an estimated 84 percent of its population living in cities today. This urban growth in North America has taken place at one and a half times the rate of the annual population growth. As significant as this is, it is dwarfed by the rate of urbanization taking place today in countries like China, India, and throughout the continent of Africa. The global rate of urbanization is two times that of global population growth, while in Asia it is occurring at three times the rate of its annual population growth. The human story has taken a remarkable shift from a rural way of life to an urban reality, and is continuing at a phenomenal rate.

Consequently, while the world has been moving to the cities over the last fifty years, there have been noticeable changes in the lack of church growth, especially in highly urbanized areas. Each week, 62,000 people are added to the cities in North America, yet 53,000 people a week are leaving the church. The number of Christians in North America who have faith in God, but communicate a loss of belief in the institution of the church, has doubled in the last twenty years to eighty million. We are experiencing a crisis of faith in this increasingly urban generation. It is not a crisis of faith in God, but an increasing struggle with the church's perceived lack of ability to speak the language of an urban culture. While America grew from 64 percent urban to 84 percent urban in the last fifty years, it experienced only a 2 percent church growth rate. Not only has virtually all that growth existed outside urban areas, but is not even keeping up with the average annual growth rate of the country. If the trend continues, it's estimated that in ten years only 14 percent of Americans will attend church; by 2050, it could be less than 10 percent.

Is it possible there is a connection between the growing numbers leaving church culture and the growing numbers of those moving to and existing in cities? Over the last twenty years of talking to people on the streets of Chicago, I have observed some common trends of spiritual struggle and lack of faith in the church. I believe it would be a mistake to conclude that this urban-connected generation lacks spirituality or the desire to commit to God. In actuality, I have experienced an increasing spiritual hunger and passion among believers and nonbelievers alike. We have surveyed and prayed with thousands of people in Chicago over the years. Not only do I find more and more people pursuing spirituality and communities of faith outside organized church, but I hear a growing perception that the established church is losing identification and validity with an urban-saturated world.

The implications of these perceptions not only affect church growth, but also affect those ministries that seek to attract, equip, and mobilize the current generation into global mission. We may be losing our ability to attract the current generation simply because we are perceived as no longer having anything of relevance to say. There are incredible giftings and passions in this urban generation to transform nations. But their struggle with the church and those connected with historical Christianity is leaving them without an inheritance, directionless, and without a clear call of leadership into the urban world of the twenty-first century. I would like to suggest that an urban worldview has emerged over the last few decades that is influencing how this generation views God and processes truth in general. The implications of this increasing global worldview are affecting the church and those of us who seek to mobilize and equip the church into world mission. Below are some of the significant ways that this generation is looking at and processing reality.

THE HUMAN STORY IS BROKEN

This urban-connected generation is personally aware of brokenness. The city does not create new forms of brokenness; it simply magnifies, multiplies, and accentuates it. Injustice, gross poverty, violence, and family breakdown are normal, daily realities to the urban dweller. The deep cry has become, "Where is God?" Because of technology and globalization, this generation struggles with the real and felt presence of suffering around the world. They are overwhelmed not just with the suffering in their own lives, but the inability to ignore the realities of global pain and suffering. The suffering debate is no longer why evil exists, but where is God and what does He want to do in response to evil? This generation is looking to the church to not merely teach a theology of survival but a message of redemption. Some of the questions being asked are, "Can the broken human story be fixed?" and "Can we be equipped by God to make real change?"

There is a deep cry to reclaim the image of God over humanity. In order to identify with this cry, the church must be at the forefront of those who display frustration over every disruption of God's original intent for the world. The passion of the church must go beyond simply an individual application of God's redeeming grace to include corporate expressions of redemption over all of the complexities of the human story. In order to attract the hunger and attention of this generation, we must begin to speak louder than the world on issues of injustice, the vandalism of human dignity, and our need to steward God's creation properly. We do not need to lessen our commitment to the truth of individual salvation. However, unless the world perceives that we are burdened by the brokenness of all of God's dreams for humanity, our vision is seen as too small and irrelevant.

We may find it easy to convince the urban world that God is not the author of evil. They accept this, often more readily than some in the religious community. They are aware of evil in humanity. They want to know if God just left us or does He fight for us. The message of Romans 8:37–39 is an important message for our time. Suffering and evil will not separate us from God's commitment to our highest good and do not have to derail His purpose for our lives. Truth is now made relevant to the degree it speaks adequately and displays action steps toward human suffering. The churches and ministries who will draw the attention of a twenty-first century urban world will be those who are perceived as addressing the broken human story with identification, compassion, and real action towards repairing, reclaiming, and restoring God's vision for humanity.

DIVERSITY WITH UNITY AND PURPOSE IS NOT ONLY A VALUE BUT A NECESSITY

The urban world is experiencing a level of diversity that has not previously been seen in the human story. Many cities in North America house over half of the world's nationalities. In a five-mile radius in Chicago, there are over 150 nationalities. The students of the public schools speak over 100 languages natively. The urbanization of the developing world is bringing hundreds of people groups and dialects out of rural isolation into concentrated urban neighborhoods. This generation is hungry for an example of diverse community, experiencing true unity and synergistic purpose. Truth is being validated to the degree that it can exist in the context of diverse interrelating community. Diversity is an everyday reality for the city dweller. This reinforces the crisis of faith many are feeling toward the church.

While 84 percent of North America is living in diverse urban realities, 92.5 percent of churches in North America are "monoracial," in which 80 percent or more of the church is made up of the same ethnicity or race.[1] It is considered the most segregated institution in our culture. It begs the question, "Where is the true family of God?" Our message of truth is being tested by how well it is connected to, and survives, diversity. This generation is experiencing more diverse interrelating in coffee bars and public institutions than in church. The need to find purpose for diversity is a necessity and deep cry for the urban world. The church must show vision and leadership in this area. We will attract this generation to the degree that we have moved from simply valuing diversity to actually creating environments where it can exist with unity and synergistic purpose. John 17:20–23 not only reveals the vision of Jesus for this unity, but reminds us that it is this very characteristic of His followers that will convince the world that He truly must have come from the Father.

Church planting and missional communities must display the same diversity that the urban world sees as a reality. The God that we preach is the author of the nations and all its diversity. If we cannot give visible witness of the unity and purpose of that diversity, our message has become suspect. The urban world is reeling under racial tension and both cultural and economic segregation. They are looking to the religious community for leadership in increasingly complex and diverse communities. As we embrace this identity of diversity with unity, we will attract a growing urban generation.

Truth Is Transferred and Defined Not Through Ideology or Teaching but In and Through People's Lives

Urban life is pragmatic, not ideological. The global urban culture is saturated with philosophy, trends, and options of spirituality. The urban dweller is in an overload of options, all being advertised as the one true way to success and meaning. This generation is attracted by what is perceived as effectually working. Truth must now be seen, tasted, and touched; not merely heard. Linear transference of truth is no longer valued. Rather, truth is accepted through relational and experiential contact. It is not coming from an unwillingness to operate in faith, but a deep cry for genuineness and a spirituality that actually produces something. The question is, "Where are the true Sons of God?"

According to the Barna research group, 85 percent of twenty-four million nonbelievers in North America know at least five Christians; yet only 15 percent say that those Christians display any difference in lifestyle from those who are not Christian.[2] The implication is that we need a new setting for our classroom. We need to live out our message in the most complex environments of the urban world. We need to create an incarnational and physical context to our teaching and discipleship. Jesus made physical application the context for revealing truth when He put on flesh and dwelt among us so that we could see His glory (John 1:14). It's not that our message is no longer valid, but rather it is being validated by how well we are living it out in the context by which the majority of the world exists today. If we continue to present our message and discipleship only from a rural, suburban, or homogeneous context, it will increasingly be suspect in a world no longer relating to that reality.

The examples of our message cannot be simply taught, but must be seen. In John 14:6, Jesus took the revelation of truth out of the context of teaching into the physical reality of a person. The urban world hungers to see the person of Jesus. The churches and ministries that will draw the attention of this twenty-first century generation will be those who are connected in some way to the context of struggle and reality in the urban world. This generation is so desperate to find instant application to the urban reality that they no longer want to be taught through the method of removal from the world, but rather in the midst of it. They want to be taught in the marketplace.

Our need to influence and exist in the spheres of society is no longer simply for evangelistic reasons, but so that truth can be validated by how well it works in the world. Many in this generation no longer want to experience church and discipleship monastically or from safe, isolated structures, but rather in corporate offices, high-rise apartment buildings, slums, and street corners. They are redefining church to be something that exists through community, no matter where it takes place, and not in buildings. We must take our worship and processes of discipleship public in order to remain relevant.

Value Is Placed Not on Structure but Movement and That Which Effects Change

The urban world is intense and complex. Spirituality is no longer seen as a personal thing. Every social issue is seen as a spiritual issue. This urban generation is looking for a spirituality that produces change in the world around it. The question being asked is, "Are we going anywhere?" No longer are churches or ministries validated by how well established or how big they are. The urban view is the perception that the world is slanted toward the rich and the powerful. If a church or ministry is big, it is actually suspected of running over somebody to get there.

Structures are not valued in and of themselves, but only to the degree that they are creating movement and real change. They are hungering for real movement that inspires, and they are ready to sacrifice their lives for true causes. They are simply not impressed with institutions. They want to join something that looks grassroots, organic, and very relationally connected to humanity.

Our very existence as a church or ministry is being validated by how much change we are creating in the world, and how personally connected we are toward that world we seek to impact. We will attract this generation to the degree that they feel we are touching real need. They do not want gated Christian community, but rather messy, integrated, relationally risky involvement with the world. John 15:8 reminds us that the world will believe Jesus has come from the Father by the fruit we produce. The implication is that the church will need to recapture the method of discipleship that Jesus used, by inviting people to discover God, discipleship, and spiritual maturity while doing ministry in the world. Again, this generation wants to discover spirituality through action and integration into the world, rather than removal from it. They must feel that we are so radically going somewhere that they will miss out if they do not jump on board.

As we move into the twenty-first century, the conclusion is that its level of urban connectedness will increasingly validate the church. Our voice will only be heard and respected to the degree we are identifying with and touching the heart cry of an urban generation. The urban world will only be reached by embracing the parable Jesus gave in Matthew 13:31–34. He reminded us that the kingdom of God (the physical application of the ways of God's rule) would affect the world like leaven (or ferment) in a loaf of bread. To ferment literally means to infect and change a substance at the cellular level. We must dramatically and physically connect with the complex increasing urban realities of our world in order to infect it on a cellular level. As we do this, the church, and those ministries seeking to equip and mobilize the church, will be both validated and heard, attracting an urban generation that has the heart, hunger, and ability to change the world.

BIBLIOGRAPHY

Bakke, Ray. *A Theology as Big as the City*. Downers Grove, IL: InterVarsity Press, 1997.

Bakke, Ray. *The Urban Christian*. Downers Grove, IL: InterVarsity Press, 1987.

Barna, George. *Revolution*. Carol Stream, IL: Tyndale House, 2005.

Conn, Harvie M. *A Clarified Vision for Urban Mission*. Grand Rapids, MI: Zondervan, 1987.

Conn, Harvie M., and Manuel Ortiz. *Urban Ministry: The Kingdom, the City, & the People of God*. Downers Grove, IL: InterVarsity Press, 2001.

Cunningham, Sarah. *Dear Church: Letters from a Disillusioned Generation*. Grand Rapids, MI: Zondervan, 2006.

Dawson, John. *Taking Our Cities for God*. Lake Mary, FL: Charisma House, 2001.

Dennison, Jack. *City Reaching: On the Road to Community Transformation*. Pasadena, CA: William Carey Library, 1999.

DeYmaz, Mark. *Building a Healthy Multi-Ethnic Church*. San Francisco: Jossey-Bass, 2007.

Emerson, Michael O., and Christian Smith. *Divided by Faith: Evangelical Religion and the Problem of Race in America*. New York: Oxford University Press, 2000.

Fuder, John. *A Heart for the City: Effective Ministries to the Urban Community*. Chicago: Moody Press, 1999.

Fuder, John, and Noel Castellanos. *A Heart for the Community: New Models for Urban and Suburban Ministry*. Chicago: Moody Press, 2009.

Greenway, Roger S. *Apostles to the City: Biblical Strategies for Urban Missions.* Grand Rapids, MI: Baker Books, 1978.

Halter, Hugh, and Matt Smay. *The Tangible Kingdom: Creating Incarnational Community.* San Francisco: Jossey-Bass, 2008.

Kinnaman, David. *UnChristian: What a New Generation Really Thinks About Christianity and Why It Matters.* Grand Rapids, MI: Baker Books, 2007.

McClung, Floyd. *Seeing the City with the Eyes of God: How Christians Can Rise to the Urban Challenge.* Grand Rapids, MI: Chosen Books, 1991.

Meeks, Wayne A. *The First Urban Christians: The Social World of the Apostle Paul.* New Haven, CT: Yale University Press, 1983.

Perkins, John M. *Restoring at-Risk Communities.* Grand Rapids, MI: Baker Books, 1995.

Stier, Jim, Richlyn Poor, and Lisa Orvis. *His Kingdom Come: An Integrated Approach to Discipling the Nations and Fullfilling the Great Commission.* Seattle: YWAM Publishing, 2008.

NOTES

INTRODUCTION

1. United Nations Department of Economic and Social Affairs, "World Urbanization Prospects: The 2009 Revision," 3.

2. Harvie M. Conn and Manuel Ortiz, *Urban Ministry: The Kingdom, the City, & the People of God* (Downers Grove, IL: InterVarsity Press, 2001), 26.

3. BBC News, Urban Planet. http://news.bbc.co.uk/2/hi/in_depth/world/2006/urbanisation/default.stm (accessed August 16, 2011).

4. United Nations, "World Urbanization Prospects," 3.

5. Ibid., 1.

6. Conn and Ortiz, 17.

7. Erla Zwingle, "Cities: Challenges for Humanity," *National Geographic*, November 2002 issue, 78.

8. United Nations, "World Urbanization Prospects," 4.

9. Zwingle, 76.

10. United Nations, "World Urbanization Prospects," 6.

11. Malcolm Moore and Peter Foster, "China to Create Largest Mega City in the World with 42 Million People," *The Telegraph*, January 24, 2011, http://www.telegraph.co.uk/news/worldnews/asia/china/8278315/China-to-create-largest-mega-city-in-the-world-with-42-million-people.html (accessed August 16, 2011).

12. Ibid., 6 (the U.N. report).

13. Conn and Ortiz, 19.

14. Although the developing world of Asia and Africa was still 75 percent or more rural populations, there were already cities in India and China beginning to reach numbers of one to five million.

CHAPTER 1: THE MISSIONARY GOD

1. Conn and Ortiz, 25.

2. James Strong, *A Concise Dictionary of the Words in the Hebrew Bible; with their renderings in the Authorized English Version* (1890), s.v. *machashabah* (H4284).

3. Ibid., s.v. *genea* (G1074).

4. Ibid., s.v. *idios* (G2398).

5. Ibid., s.v. *dunamis* (G1411).

6. Ibid., s.v. *idios* (G2398).

CHAPTER 2: THE FALLEN CITY

1. Floyd McClung, *Seeing the City with the Eyes of God: How Christians Can Rise to Urban Challenge* (Grand Rapids, MI: Chosen Books, 1991) 63.

2. Zwingle, 92.

3. Tracy Swartz, "Chicago sees 448 homicides in 2010," *RedEye*, January 6, 2011, http://www.chicagonow.com/blogs/redeye/2011/01/chicago-sees-448-homicides-in-2010.html (accessed August 16, 2011).

4. John Dawson, *Taking Our Cities for God* (Lake Mary, FL: Charisma House, 2001), 99.

CHAPTER 3: LOOKING FOR HOME

1. McClung, 65.

2. Strong's Greek Dictionary, s.v. *polis* (G4172).

3. Ibid., s.v. *ekdechomai* (G1551).

4. Ibid., s.v. *oikia* (G3614).

5. Ibid., s.v. *mone* (G3438).

6. Ibid., s.v. *meno* (G3306).

7. Ibid., s.v. *topos* (G5117).

8. Ibid., s.v. *chora* (G5561).

CHAPTER 4: GETTING CLOSE TO GOD

1. Dawson, 129.

2. Strong's Greek Dictionary, s.v. *poiema* (G4161).

3. Strong's Hebrew Dictionary, s.v. *shakan* (H7931).

4. Ibid., s.v. *dakka'* (H1793).

5. Ibid., s.v. *shaphal* (H8217).

Chapter 5: The Nations Are Coming

1. Ray Bakke, *A Theology as Big as the City* (Downers Grove, IL: InterVarsity Press, 1997), 13.

2. Alexander Russo, "Immigrant Student Faces Language, Social Hurdles," Catalyst Chicago, February 2006, http://www.catalyst-chicago.org/news/index.php?item=1914&cat=23 (accessed August 16, 2011).

3. Jason P. Schachter, Rachel S. Franklin, and Marc J. Perry, "Migration and Geographic Mobility in Metropolitan and Non-metropolitan America: 1995 to 2000," U.S. Census Bureau, August 2003, http://www.census.gov/prod/2003pubs/censr-9.pdf (accessed August 16, 2011).

4. Nathan P. Walters and Rachel T. Cortes, "Year of Entry of the Foreign-Born Population: 2009," U.S. Census Bureau, October 2010, http://www.census.gov/prod/2010pubs/acsbr09-17.pdf (accessed August 16, 2011).

5. Schachter, Franklin, and Perry.

6. United Nations International Migration Report 2002, Department of Economic and Social Affairs, http://www.un.org/esa/population/publications/ittmig2002/2002ITTMIGTEXT22-11.pdf (accessed August 16, 2011).

7. Marie Price and Lisa Benton-Short, "Counting Immigrants in Cities across the Globe," George Washington University, January 2007, http://www.migrationinformation.org/Feature/display.cfm?ID=567 (accessed August 16, 2011).

8. Schachter, Franklin, and Perry.

9. Ibid.

10. Ibid.

11. Elizabeth M. Grieco and Edward N. Trevelyan, "Place of Birth of the Foreign-Born Population: 2009," U.S. Census Bureau, October 2010, http://www.census.gov/prod/2010pubs/acsbr09-15.pdf (accessed August 16, 2011).

12. Ibid.

13. United Nations, "World Urbanization Prospects," 3.

CHAPTER 6: RELEASING A NEW MISSIONS GIFT

1. Dawson, 22.

2. Institute of International Education, "International Student Enrollments Rose Modestly in 2009/10, Led by Strong Increase in Students from China," November 15, 2010, http://www.iie.org/en/Who-We-Are/News-and-Events/Press-Center/Press-Releases/2010/2010-11-15-Open-Doors-International-Students-In-The-US (accessed August 16, 2011).

3. "The Jesus Film Project," A Ministry of Campus Crusade for Christ, http://www.jesusfilm.org/ (accessed August 16, 2011).

CHAPTER 7: A PLACE FOR HEALING

1. Roger S. Greenway, *Apostles to the City: Biblical Strategies for Urban Missions* (Grand Rapids, MI: Baker Books, 1978), 35.

2. Dawson, 29.

3. Information about Prayer Stations can be found at http://www.ywamny.org/programs/prayer-stations

4. Strong's Greek Dictionary, s.v. *splagchnizomai* (G4697).

CHAPTER 8: RIDING THE NEW WAVE OF MISSIONS

1. Greenway, 26.

2. Strong's Greek Dictionary, s.v. *ethnarches* (G1484).

3. Ibid., s.v. *epecho* (G907).

4. Ralph D. Winter, "Four Men, Three Eras, Two Transitions: Modern Missions," in *Perspectives on the World Christian Movement* (Pasadena, CA: William Carey Library 1999), 253.

5. Ibid., 258.

6. Ibid., 260

7. Jim Stier, Richlyn Poor, and Lisa Orvis, *His Kingdom Come: An Integrated Approach to Discipling the Nations and*

Fullfilling the Great Commission (Seattle: YWAM Publishing, 2008).

8. Dawson, 17.

Chapter 9: Filling the Earth with His Glory

1. Jack Dennison, *City Reaching: On the Road to Community Transformation* (Pasadena, CA: William Carey Library, 1999), 114.

2. Strong's Hebrew Dictionary, s.v. *kabowd* (H3519).

Chapter 10: The Secrets of the Kingdom

1. Dennison, 106.

2. Ibid.

3. Strong's Greek Dictionary, s.v. *ekgrupto* (G1470).

4. *Noah Webster's 1828 American Dictionary*, s.v. "Leaven," http://www.1828-dictionary.com/d/search/word,leaven, (accessed August 16, 2011).

5. Ibid., s.v. "Incarnation," http://www.1828-dictionary.com/d/search/word,incarnation (accessed August 16, 2011).

Appendix: An Urban Worldview and Its Implications for Church and Missions

1. Mark DeYmaz, *Building a Healthy Multi-Ethnic Church* (San Francisco: Jossey-Bass, 2007), 4.

2. David Kinnaman, *UnChristian: What a New Generation Really Thinks About Christianity and Why It Matters* (Grand Rapids, MI: Baker Books, 2007), 48.

ABOUT THE AUTHOR

B RAD STANLEY IS currently the Director of Youth
With A Mission Chicago. He has served as a full-
time missionary for the last 25 years, which has
taken him to more than 20 nations. For the past 19 years he
has worked to develop and train city ministry in Chicago,
with a special emphasis on cross-cultural ministry among
urban immigrant and sub-culture neighborhoods. Brad
speaks regularly in churches and mission training schools
both in the U.S. and abroad. He is directly involved in
facilitating hundreds of volunteers each year in urban
and international outreach endeavors as well as training
urban missionaries. Brad is also the author of Unwilling
to Concede, which after the loss of his wife and ministry
partner to cancer in 2003, chronicles the lessons he and
his kids learned of God's redeeming commitment toward
finishing His purposes in our lives in spite of our loss and
brokenness.

You can follow Brad's ministry at www.ywamchicago.org
and on their ywamchicago Facebook page.

CONTACT THE AUTHOR

WWW.FINDINGGODINTHECITY.COM